# Young Children Learning

# Young Children Learning

# Discovering the Physical World

## Alice Yardley

Principal Lecturer in Education,
Nottingham College of Education

Evans Brothers Limited, London

Published by Evans Brothers Limited
Montague House, Russell Square, London, W.C.1

First published 1970
Reprinted 1971, 1973, 1974

The following are the four titles in the
YOUNG CHILDREN LEARNING series by Alice Yardley:

REACHING OUT

EXPLORATION AND LANGUAGE

DISCOVERING THE PHYSICAL WORLD

SENSES AND SENSITIVITY

Also by Alice Yardley:

THE TEACHER OF YOUNG CHILDREN

YOUNG CHILDREN THINKING

LEARNING TO ADJUST

THE INFANT SCHOOL

Cover photograph : Will Green

Printed in Great Britain by T. and A. Constable Ltd..
Hopetoun Street, Edinburgh.

ISBN 0 237 28645 9                    PRA 3760

# Contents

# Introduction

This book is basically an examination of the way in which children begin to develop mathematical and scientific ideas. The way in which experience contributes to the formation of concepts is illustrated by the observations of teachers whose aim it was to promote the child's study and understanding of his physical environment.

Exploration is the way a child lives, and the world of today abounds in opportunities to investigate not only natural phenomena but also the complexities of technical phenomena in an environment where so much is made by man. The aim of the teacher is to ensure sound development of basic mathematical and scientific ideas. The child can scarcely avoid imbibing scientific ideas and language, but he will absorb these more effectively if he shares the experience with an adult who understands. Learning goes on all the time, but the perceptive adult can direct the child's attention more closely towards the mathematical and scientific aspects of his physical world.

The teacher provides an adequate supply of basic material and so ensures the opportunity to learn at first hand. If her own knowledge of the material is good, curiosity is quickened and the child's opportunities for discovery are broadened. Good basic material consists largely of homely equipment

7

with which the child is fully familiar, so that the child's attention is focused on situations he already comprehends; these provide a starting-point for enquiry at greater depth.

None of the teachers whose work is quoted were either mathematicians or scientists. They were all women teachers, many of them married with children of their own, who made the effort to acquaint themselves more fully with their surroundings. Time and time again, the spontaneous curiosity of the children they taught re-enthused them and they discovered within themselves unexplored powers of understanding. Sometimes they made mistakes and occasionally drew faulty conclusions, but the quality of conceptual development in their children overwhelmingly compensated for a few minor errors. Teachers whose powers of mathematical and scientific thought are undeveloped may feel encouraged by these records to adventure themselves into the child's wonderful world of discovery. They may find unexpected problems and encounter disastrous episodes, but they will be amply rewarded as the vital nature of learning at first hand becomes fully evident.

# 1

# The need to explore

At birth the child is thrust into the unknown. If he is to survive he must find out about the world into which he is born, he must learn to understand it and so come to terms with it. In the early stages the child has no words and cannot learn by being told. He depends entirely on his own resources, and these resources are his curiosity, his ability to reach out and manipulate, and the use of his senses as a means of conveying information to his brain. He does not have to be taught how to be curious, and it is through his innate urge to explore that he learns to survive.

Not only is learning essential, it gives great joy to the young child. Everything within reach delights him, and existence for him is the sheer pleasure of knowing that he is alive, and alive in a world full of exciting things awaiting his discovery. At first his world extends as far as he can reach, and the satisfaction of his physical needs is his main interest in it. The speed of his learning depends on the amount of freedom he has to explore. As he becomes more mobile his world expands, and the acquisition of words opens up a new kind of exploration.

The growth of the child's understanding is a twofold process: exploration enables him to order his world of external things, and at the same time his inner world of the mind is taking shape. The organisation of the external and the internal

9

world makes them complementary aspects of the same process. As the child explores, his mind grows and his developing mind enables him to understand.

The child's first and most permanent source of information is his skin. The most sensitive part of his skin is where it enters openings into the body. The baby's exploration starts in his mouth and he will continue to examine the properties of objects with his mouth for a number of years.

Later he will learn how to see and to hear and to smell. Experience will teach him how to interpret messages received through his eyes and his ears. He will, for instance, learn to perceive the three-dimensional shape of his cup after he has discovered its solidity through handling it. In later life the senses of seeing and hearing may diminish. He may even be deprived of the use of them and still survive, but complete loss of the sense of touch would make learning and living virtually impossible. So fundamental is the child's need to handle that 'Don't touch' is equivalent to 'Don't learn', and in the early stages the child's knowing and understanding depend on his feeling things.

By the time the child enters school he has discovered much about his world. He has discovered his own body and has some idea of himself. He knows a good deal about the objects in his environment, about the behaviour of materials such as water and soil and sand. He knows something of the nature of air and light and sound.

His need to manipulate and examine the unfamiliar may lead to observation with interest. He will try to describe what he sees and find ways of measuring it. He will enquire further about it. At a later stage he can learn to measure and to record his discoveries systematically. This exploration and enquiry associated with accurate observation and systematic recording are the beginning of science. The ordering of his findings and the measurement of his observations are the beginnings of mathematical understanding.

Throughout the Primary School years the child will continue to rely on sensory experiences for information and meaning. He feels the sharp grittiness of the sand. He sees it sift through the holes in the sieve. He hears its staccato patter as it falls on paper. He discovers what it will and will not do, and what he can do with it as he manipulates it, sometimes dry, sometimes wet. Each of these experiences is associated with his emotional state at the time: joy, excitement, pleasure, satisfaction, and perhaps the pain of sand in his eyes and the fear of its vast expanse when seen for the first time on the beach. Sensory and emotional experiences become linked in understanding. These early impressions are powerful and lasting, for early sensory and emotional experiences colour the view adults hold of things.

The child who is free to explore and is encouraged to do so has adequate opportunity for learning. The child who is restricted and expected to learn in an arid classroom will learn very slowly. Likewise the classroom filled with objects which only the teacher is allowed to handle is a poor learning situation. The child must be free to explore with his hands, and meaning develops through the things he does with his materials. The materials themselves will educate. The teacher's words may help the child to explore more effectively, but nothing can supersede his first-hand experiences.

Most children when confronted with new materials go through two stages in their discovery of them. Whether presented with sand or clay, with words or numbers, with sounds or colours, children need first to experiment to discover the nature and discipline of the various materials. They may then leave them alone for a while and only later return to them with some clear object in mind.

This procedure sometimes dismays teachers. From the adult point of view, the initial 'messing about' produces nothing and is therefore useless. These exciting materials have failed, or so it seems, to inspire creative use of them.

There are no results. Yet such apparently fruitless early stages are essential to understanding. It is then that the child discovers the properties of his materials, and the ultimate quality of his creative work depends on the relationship made by the child with these materials as he explores them. The child's exploration and creative use of materials are both ways of understanding them.

It is important to remember, too, that the real world and the fantasy life of the young child are closely associated. When confronted with an unfamiliar situation he will accept magical explanations. A six-year-old enjoyed the happy yellow of primroses in the garden in daylight. When he saw them at dusk their colour had gone. 'The darkness has taken the colour away', he explained.

Hugh was given a watch with luminous figures on a black dial. He pondered over it for some time and then decided: 'Black dissolves light and does not let it out again.' Speculating in this way is a form of reasoning and sometimes nearly a factual explanation. What is more, children remain well aware of the difference between the real and the fantasy world. The explanations they devise are recognised as satisfactory only for the time being. It is as though children realise that their understanding is immature and will deepen as experience teaches them.

Once a child has acquired facts he enjoys playing with them, and using facts imaginatively is a firm indication that the child has really made them his own. It is only when facts are thoroughly familiar that he becomes able to play about with them in imagination.

Facts and information are useless to the child unless he understands and his ability to understand is a measure of his mental development. The child begins to understand as soon as he begins to discriminate. A baby of three weeks will unexpectedly focus his attention on the woolly ball bobbing from the canopy of his pram. For an instant he becomes aware of it as different from the rest of his environment. Later he will discriminate between people, between objects, between sounds, and between his emotions. He will recognise the relationship between a new experience and an old one. He can begin to speculate, anticipating a future situation, basing his deductions on past experience. A four-year-old was told by his mother: 'We must go to the bank on the way to the shops.' He fetched pencil and paper and began to scribble: 'I'm going to buy money like Daddy.'

This growing ability to reason and to understand helps the child to explore and to learn from his discoveries. What he observes means something to him and the understanding which follows is far more important to the child than memorising. Modern classroom procedure recognises the living quality of the discovery approach to learning. What the child personally discovers has meaning for him, and he knows it; merely memorising the written or spoken fact provides only superficial understanding.

When teaching was thought of in terms of teacher-directed work aimed at producing set standards of achievement, the job of the teacher was comparatively easy. Today we recognise the great importance of child-initiated activity and the necessity for the child to learn as an individual with unique needs and unique modes of satisfying them.

When we provide materials calculated to stimulate the child's curiosity we put ourselves in a very difficult position. We do not decide in advance exactly what the child shall discover and we expose ourselves to questions which tax and sometimes baffle us. The child does not stop to ask whether his teacher is a scientist or a mathematician – he simply asks extremely awkward questions.

How can teachers gain enough confidence to put themselves in this situation? Just knowing a few facts or formulae doesn't help much. Knowing the answer is in itself a barrier to further thinking. As adults we have stopped asking such important questions as why sugar dissolves when sand doesn't and why face powder clings to the skin. We are in a better position to help the child in his discovery when we face ourselves with basic problems and learn to look with the fresh eyes of a child at familiar materials. By so doing we become more aware and discover ways in which we can improve our own inadequate concepts of science or mathematics. The enthusiasm and awareness of the teacher affect the work of the children profoundly, and as our awareness grows so does theirs. Knowing what the child *can* discover enables us to guide him in his discovery. We know the right questions to ask him, the right piece of equipment to add to the situation, the right reference book to refer him to, and so we lead him on in the direction he has chosen.

As teachers our job is first to provide materials which will stimulate and reward curiosity, then to help the child to observe accurately and later record with precision, to organise his information so that it shall be of use to him, and to measure with great care what he observes. Scientific observation and mathematical assessment will lead to profitable and creative discovery.

We know, too, that the effects of any experience neither begin nor end with that experience. The child brings to each situation all that he is as a person. How he deals with a situation depends on the type of person he is and how far he has gone in his personal development. The experience itself effects a change in the child as it becomes built into his person. Every experience becomes in some way part of him. As any one of us stands at this moment, the personality of each is the sum total of all that has happened to us.

By giving the child vital opportunities to discover his world and adjust to it, teachers and parents ensure the full and satisfactory development of his personality. This enrichment of day-to-day living ensures that the child lives life to the full.

# 2

# The development of mathematical thinking

Mathematical understanding has roots in the child's earliest experiences. We no longer think that learning mathematics is reserved for the Secondary School and based on a little simple arithmetic taught at the Primary stage. Recent research has shown us that the development of logical thinking is an inward process which evolves through a predictable sequence of stages and that the structuring of the mind starts at birth and is a slow continuous opening-up of initial potential.

Mathematics exists only in the mind. It happens as the mind seeks to classify objects in the environment and impose order on them. It is created by each individual and can be applied to any situation. The quality of mathematical thought in an individual depends on the quality of his mind.

The creative nature of mathematics means that there is no one mathematics. It varies according to the people who create it, and each society has its own set of ideas. A child born into any particular social group inherits the ideas of that group. The ordered world of his social environment has been determined by his forefathers, and exploration of the world he is born into leads him to the discovery of their ideas.

A generation ago society expected the school to train children to calculate quickly and accurately. Automation has dispensed with the human computer and society today needs the man who can think, who can create problems as well as help solve them.

Developmental psychologists have in recent years emphasised the twofold nature of intellectual growth. 'There are two determinants of intellectual growth: a completely necessary innate potential and a completely necessary stimulating environment' (D. O. Hebb, *The Organisation of Behaviour*). As teachers we recognise our responsibility in providing a vital environment. We no longer believe that innate intelligence will develop unaided; we know that it needs good soil to unfold and thrive in.

Piaget devoted a lifetime to the study of the way in which children learn to think. He devised a wide range of experiments to investigate the beginnings of number notions in the mind of the child. He pointed out that the growth of the mind is an inward process unfolding through a sequence of stages, and that a child has to learn from personal experience how to think. He warns us against assuming that, because a child uses the language of adults and seems to learn to speak as they do, he thinks in the same way. He alerts us to the fact that a child may use a term correctly in one situation, but his understanding of the term may be limited to that situation alone and he may be quite unaware of the full range of its meaning.

A child of four, for instance, may describe the shape of an orange as round. He may remain for some time quite unable to extend his idea of roundness to include the shape of a penny or a cocoa-tin, and such terms as 'a round dozen' or 'round off the party' will remain incomprehensible to him for some years to come. The formation of concepts is a much slower process than one would suppose, and what seems simple common sense to the adult is frequently beyond the reasoning power of the child.

Peter, a normally intelligent boy of six and a half, was acting as shopkeeper. 'Your biscuits are a penny each,' his teacher observed. 'How many can I have for sixpence?' Peter hesitated and then offered a handful. 'A lot,' he suggested. It was not a foregone conclusion to Peter that because he gave one biscuit in exchange for one penny, he would give six for a sixpenny-bit or even in exchange for six pennies. He could only learn from personal experience that letting one biscuit correspond to each penny led to the idea that six biscuits would correspond to six pennies.

The development of the child's inner mental structures depends on his capacity to respond to experiences, to organise and to learn from them. Each child follows a predictable pattern of development, proceeding through a series of stages, but there are considerable differences in the chronological ages at which these stages are reached.

Piaget described three stages of mental development as taking place between birth and about the age of seven or eight. In his first weeks the baby is unaware of permanent objects outside of himself. His growing idea of himself as an independent person enables him to see himself in relation to objects in his environment. He develops a sense of space and of the shape of himself and of other objects. As he develops the use of language he begins to understand relationships between himself and other people. He begins to realise that his is not the only point of view, that all the objects in the world are related to other people besides himself, and that he is only part of a pattern. At this stage the child can perform actions and begins to form notions of objects, and he can imagine them even when they are not in view. He will 'remember' where mother keeps the chocolate biscuits, or will look in the cupboard for a favourite toy (see *Exploration and Language* in this series, Chapter 5).

During the second stage, from about eighteen months or two years up to four years, the child begins to use symbols and can carry images of actions in his mind; he can imitate actions by imagining them instead of doing them if need be. He

17

develops his use of words but needs to associate them with his own actions or objects he knows. He may, for instance, call every woman he meets 'Mam-mam', or the word 'two' may be used as the name for any number of objects. At the same time he remains unable to distinguish between subjective and objective, and if he bangs his head against the sideboard he will believe that the sideboard feels it too.

Between the ages of about four and seven or eight, the child's thought becomes more organised, although he still depends on what he sees. He will watch his teacher spread a palmful of small sweets over a table-top and declare that there are more of them when spread out than when collected in her hand. Children at this stage *can* reason, but many factors influence their decisions. Deirdre, aged five, was shown a row of six houses in a picture. She was given the numbers 1 to 6 and asked to number the row. Although she knew each number and its place in sequence, she selected the number 3 and placed it on the first house 'because,' she explained, 'I live at number three and I like that number best.'

Towards the end of this stage, by about the age of seven-plus, the child is capable of making classifications, of seeing relations and of ordering (Chapter 4). He has, moreover, formed a number of basic concepts, and once a concept is formed and has become part of the child's thinking, the process of reversibility becomes possible. By reversibility we mean the ability to return in thought to one's starting-point. This is a fundamental skill in reasoning. The child of five may give two crayons from his box of six to the next child and have no confidence in the box having six as before when the two are returned. By the time he is six, experience has taught him that with the two restored he has six again. He may be seven before he can use this idea in calculation.

From about the age of seven the child enters a further stage and is ready to use abstract ideas, to begin to reason and to speculate, but it is not until the child is about eleven years old that his powers of reasoning are fully developed and he is able to form hypotheses, make assumptions and draw conclusions from them.

Piaget labelled each of these stages, but the words he uses have very selective meanings and his terms can be misleading unless we are quite certain of the meaning he attaches to them. Thus he uses the term *sensori-motor period* for the 0- to 2-year stage, the *pre-conceptual stage* for the 2- to 4-year period, and the *stage of intuitive thinking* for the 4- to 7- or 8-year period. These last two stages form a period of preparation for the *concrete-operational stage* from seven or eight years onward. By about the age of eleven years, the child enters the *period of formal operations* or of *abstract thought*. Examples which illustrate this unfolding of thought processes will be traced in detail in Chapter 5.

Piaget's story of intellectual growth is supported by the work of a number of equally interesting research workers. Susan Isaacs, recording observations in her school in Cambridge, drew similar conclusions. Working in a different field, Ronald Goldman traces the slow development of spiritual thought and ideas. Professor Tanner sees the mind as a system which develops as part of the total pattern of organic development. Dr Lovell, Professor Peel and many others have contributed much to our understanding of the way in which children learn to think and reason. These and other workers have published results which indicate that there are differences in individual development which Piaget's approach does not reveal; we should not, therefore, accept Piaget's theories as complete.

We may summarise the conclusions reached by these people as follows:

1. The development of mathematical thought is a slow process and children learn how to think through what they do.

2. As adults we think and reason in different ways, yet our mental structures have evolved through a series of stages and as individuals we have followed similar patterns of development.

3. The rate of development is influenced considerably by the quality of experiences a child meets in his environment.

4. Once a concept has been understood, practice is essential to consolidate it. Practice follows discovery and practising a skill without understanding is useless.

The implications of these findings for the teacher are manifold. The significance of the environment is emphasised, and the need for the teacher to provide varied and vital situations is shown to be of paramount importance. Readiness to learn is closely associated with wanting to, and both parents and teachers are responsible for ensuring the child's desire to learn. By offering the child material which we know will interest him, we stimulate his urge to explore. He is motivated by his own desires, and effort and intention on his part make for effective learning. We realise that instruction is a mode of teaching which places the responsibility on the teacher. The child waits to be told what to do and learns only what the teacher decides he shall. If the situation motivates the child to explore because he is curious, learning is personal to the child and is therefore purposeful. The child learns because *he* needs to, and not because someone else thinks he should.

A further responsibility for the teacher is to introduce appropriate language when the child is actively learning. In this way, adequate modes of communicating his thoughts are made available to the child, and he is able to store his experiences in the form of words as well as in images. This leads to improvement in the quality of his thinking.

The teacher needs to observe with patience the use the child makes of his material, remembering that thought grows slowly and is the result of personal manipulation. When it becomes apparent that the child has grasped an idea, the teacher must provide adequate opportunity for practice so that the idea can become established. The futility of juggling with symbols on paper before the child has gathered ideas from handling real objects is increasingly obvious. The child's time must be spent in discovering mathematics through his own efforts, while the setting down on paper of symbols which represent mental operations has come to be seen as one of many modes of recording and never as an end in itself. Fundamental to the child's mathematical education is the knowledge that concepts cannot be taught, that they arise from the child's use of objects and his appreciation of the significance of the operations he performs with them.

This pattern in the development of the child's ideas applies not only to mathematics. In much the same way the child's ideas about science or divinity, geography or history develop with the maturation of his mental abilities. The development of concepts in a number of fields will be outlined in different parts of this book. The growth of ideas about divinity will be reserved for *Senses and Sensitivity*, the fourth book in this series.

# 3

# The language of science and mathematics

Words expressing mathematical laws and ideas are part of our thinking and speech, and children come into school using the language of mathematics because they have learned it at home. They use words such as 'big' and 'little', 'fast' and 'slow', 'more', 'tall', 'millions', 'speed', 'five', but the meaning they associate with these terms is limited by their experience of them. They use them as part of their day-to-day language which they have picked up from adults, and we mustn't assume that because a child uses a word correctly in one situation he has grasped its full meaning.

A child will tell you that he has a 'speed car'. The word 'speed' may mean to' him the shape of the car, or that it goes fast, or it may simply describe the type of car. The idea of velocity hasn't even occurred to him, and the word 'speed' will gather meaning for him over a great many years.

He may in a similar way associate 'heavy' with stones and 'light' with a meringue. The concrete step is 'hard' to sit on and mother's cheek is 'soft'. There are 'corners' in the kitchen, and a ball is 'round'. When his hair grows 'long', mother cuts it 'short'.

By the time the child enters school he may know the names of many numbers. He uses them freely as part of his speech and the meaning he attaches to them is his personal decision.

He lives, for instance, at number nine and his birthday is on September the fifteenth; he goes to bed late on Friday night but he always gets to school early; on the bus we sit in twos and buy a threepenny ticket; when Daddy goes on the motorway he drives all the way at seventy and uses gallons and gallons of petrol; there are millions of stars in the sky.

He does not see these number-words as symbols to manipulate on paper. Nor do they confuse him, and indeed there is no reason why they should. We can turn him against them, however, if we force him to use them in ways which mean nothing to him and bring no satisfaction. Or we can increase his love of them by helping him to enlarge their meaning and to use them with greater precision.

Children need to talk a lot about their numbers and to know them well before they start to write them down. We can assess the extent of a child's understanding of the terms he uses by talking to him rather than by giving him sums to get right or wrong. Getting the correct answer doesn't teach the child very much about numbers, and he will learn about them only by continuing to meet them as he has met them at home, in realistic situations and as part of what he is doing.

Understanding precedes recording and comes not from telling but from personal experience and discovery. We tempt the child to explore by providing situations which challenge and intrigue him, and even then we remember that the ability to reason and to understand mathematical terms depends as much on maturity as on the opportunities provided. However richly endowed the child's environment may be, he cannot respond to what it offers until the appropriate stage in his development is reached.

We remember, too, the relationship between words and thought, and we encourage the child to talk about his experiences and discoveries as they happen.

Richard was playing with the bricks. He collected all

23

the cubes of different sizes and arranged them in a row. 'That's the little one,' he murmured. 'That goes first. And this is the most and I put it at the end. These others are all different. I can put this bigger one here and that less big next . . .'

Listening to Richard his teacher was able to assess, fairly accurately, his understanding of the words he used. She asked him to tell her what he was doing and was then able to clarify his understanding of words such as 'most' and 'different', and to add the word 'smaller' to his vocabulary.

Piaget emphasised the importance of encouraging children to talk aloud about the operations they perform as an aid to clarifying the situation and then of confirming it to themselves. Ultimately this talking to oneself becomes internal, and plays an essential part in thinking and reasoning.

Children come by their mathematical vocabulary in every kind of situation. They meet the mathematical ideas these words represent as a dimension of every aspect of life, for mathematics is rooted in everything we do. Observation is recorded in mathematical terms. Music depends on vibrations and movement involves mathematical discipline. In art we employ perspective, proportion, pattern and order, and craft requires skilful measurement. The housewife uses mathematics when she bakes, knits or makes a dress. It is at her knee that the young child meets his first mathematical words and begins to use them as part of his verbal communication with others.

Take, for instance, the child's use of the word 'two'. As a toddler he knows that he has two feet and that mother buys him a pair of shoes. The lady next door has twins and when he looks in the pram he sees two babies. As the twins grow older their father buys them a double bunk. By the time the child is four he knows that 'two' was the name of one of his birthdays, that a bicycle has two wheels and that on the television programme two people sing a duet.

By the time he enters school the child is beginning to

24

recognise that all of these things have something in common – the quality of 'two'. 'Two' then becomes an independent idea; he has abstracted it from all the situations he knows and he is ready to accept the fact that the symbol '2' stands for his idea of 'two'. When he uses the word or sees the symbol he can think of it without referring back to all the ways in which he first met the idea. All similar words in the child's vocabulary need the support of a similar range of experiences if he is to use them with understanding and if he is to be able to manipulate the concepts in his mind and combine them with other ideas. The relationship between the ideas of 'two' and 'three', for instance, is complex and comprehensible only when wide experience of each separate idea has established it.

In school the teacher can use many situations as opportunities to develop the child's mathematical language. Ann, playing with her dolls, enjoyed weighing and measuring them. Her teacher encouraged her to describe her discoveries to her friends, and later Ann wrote about her dolls. On one page she wrote, 'Teddy weighs one pound two ounces. He is one foot five inches tall. He is a big doll. I had him when I was three years old, that was three years ago.'

Verbal recording, using either the spoken or written word, is meaningful to the child and far more educative than the use of numerical symbols alone in the form of sums. Anita wrote in her baking book:

'Miss Shaw took four children to the grocers and bought the ingredients for our jam tarts. We used 8 oz. self-raising flour, 4 oz. fat, $\frac{1}{2}$ lb. jam, and we made 36 jam tarts. We bought 1 lb. self-raising flour, 1 lb. jam and 1 lb. fat and we had $\frac{1}{2}$ lb. self-raising flour, $\frac{1}{2}$ lb. jam and 12 oz. fat left over after making the jam tarts.

'If we had used 1 lb. self-raising flour, 1 lb. jam, $\frac{1}{2}$ lb. fat, we could have made 72 jam tarts and that is 6 dozen jam tarts. . . .

'Today Jill and Odarka and Nicky and I baked jam tarts.

25

The tarts went into the oven at 11 o'clock and came out at 11.15. Fifteen minutes is a quarter of an hour, and we put more jam in the tarts and we raised the price of the jam tarts.'

Good mathematical language experience is provided by shopping when it takes place in real situations with the use of real money. Exchanging cardboard coins for dummy packets which later are returned to the shelves is of little value, but there are a number of classroom situations which provide valuable shopping experience.

Lunchtime biscuits, fruit, nuts, et cetera, are sold in a number of schools. Children working in pairs can be responsible for the sales and the account book. Biscuits often vary in price; some are two a penny, some three, four, even ten a penny, and children write out their 'biscuit' tables; the efficient shopman commits his tables to memory. The profit made on a tin of biscuits can be used to purchase incidentals for the classroom. Children can accompany the teacher on a shopping expedition for paint, materials and other odds and ends. When mothers visit on Parents' Day, children can make and sell cakes and cups of tea.

Larger denominations of coins are no more difficult to handle than pennies, in fact many children find it easier to calculate in silver. Under the supervision of the teacher they can handle dinner money, bank money, party subscriptions, photograph money or the expenses of a school visit.

These are obvious occasions when mathematical language plays an essential part in the activity. Very often, however, it is in the pursuit of other objectives that such language activity arises.

Terry, aged six, was painting a picture of his day-trip to the seaside. A broad road dominated the paper. It was flanked by symbols, sometimes in elevation, sometimes in plan. 'There is the café where we had coffee,' he explained. 'And that's the petrol station where we stopped to fill up. And then we passed the race course and there was a little town, no, a village, with lots of shops . . . They were big of course, but I've made them all little so's I can get them in the picture and that means I've drawn the car little too . . .' Terry's ideas of scale and proportion were dawning. A year later he was fascinated by maps.

Five-year-old children were helping to tidy the Wendy House. They were confronted by many utensils which they were trying to fit into a biscuit box. 'That pan goes inside this one and then the littlest one goes inside that. They look the same but they fit in.' Jill had discovered that objects can vary in size yet retain the same shape. 'If we put those pans at the back corner these plates and things will go in front.' Judy was beginning to perceive the relationship between shapes and the way in which space can be used. Barry held up a large bowl. 'It's too big to go in,' he said at length. 'It will have to go on top.' He could compare the size of the bowl with the space available by using the images in his mind, and he knew without the aid of physical experience what the answer would be.

Further examples of the essential part played by language in all fields of discovery will illustrate the text throughout the remainder of this book.

# 4

# Early mathematical experiences

Many adults tend to think that counting is the first form of number activity. Parents teach three-year-old Billy to chant 'One, two, three', and when he can repeat the words in the right order they claim, 'Billy can count. Count for Grandma, Billy.' What they actually claim for Billy is that he can match groups of objects to words, whereas Billy has probably little idea of even one group of objects. Primitive man didn't use words for counting, he matched objects, letting stones, for instance, represent people, and Billy would be better employed in a similar activity, such as letting plates, spoons and serviettes stand for people and groups of people.

Sometimes the adult tries to help the child in his counting by letting him climb the stairs or set milk bottles in a row, saying the counting words as he goes along, and this in the early stages can be very confusing. When all the bottles look the same why should one be given the name 'three' and another the name 'two'? Adults tend to forget that each number word has two kinds of meaning according to whether it is used to denote the size of a group or the place of an object in sequence. The child has much to accomplish in thought before he is ready to deal with a conventional sequence of symbols in the form of counting and to answer the question 'how many?'

The child's innate urge to order and organise means that

he is by nature methodical (see *Exploration and Language*). When handling real objects even the very young child delights in sorting and grouping together those which have something in common. Grannie's button box occupies many a young child. He will set out the big buttons and the small ones, the blue ones and the red ones, the ones with two holes and the ones with four holes, the big blue ones with two holes, and so on.

In the early stages he may collect objects together simply because they seem to go together, and he may be unaware that they have a common quality. At a later stage he will approach the game with some particular criterion in mind: 'I want all the bottles with screw tops' or 'all the round tins with lids'.

At a certain stage the number of objects in a group or set becomes significant. 'Number' is one quality of sets, and sets of different sizes can be put in order. Not until this stage in understanding has been reached is the child ready to match sets with number words and to learn that adults use these words in a special order, and hence to count.

In school there are innumerable opportunities for organising material and objects, for learning to sort and classify and then to order. Sorting with some purpose in mind is of greater value to the child than being given a collection of shells and merely being told to 'sort them out'.

Shirley and John were arranging the tarts they had made. As they worked they talked.

Shirley: 'There's lemon and jam. We'll have lemon here and jam there.'

John: 'Some's bigger. We must have big ones here and little ones there. They're twopence, but those are only a penny.'

Shirley: 'We could have big jam and little jam.'

John: 'Yes. And big lemon and little lemon.'

Shirley: 'No. That won't do. I made these. We'll have Shirley's tarts and John's tarts.'

29

At this point Shirley and John were told by their teacher, 'You've spent long enough arranging those tarts. You'd better leave them and get on with your sum cards.' Too often children are hurried through vital experiences because figures on paper produce visible results. In these early stages time is more profitably spent in performing concrete operations with all kinds of objects.

In the milk crate the empty bottles can be sorted from the full bottles. The colour of the bottle-tops – gold, blue, silver, and so on – would be another criterion for sorting milk bottles. Bricks can be sorted according to shape or size or purpose. Tidying up the woodwork bench involves putting nails, screws, and other objects into their own boxes, and pieces of wood are sorted according to size. In a similar way the sewing-table or the 'make-box' provides a variety of objects which can be grouped together or classified, e.g. long or short pieces of ribbon, string, wire, round dowelling rods and flat dowelling rods, different kinds of fasteners, sewing needles and cotton reels of different sizes or colours.

Money is classified according to type of coin. Physical education equipment needs sorting into balls, bean-bags, ropes, et cetera. On the nature table, bulbs are sorted according to size and packets of bird seed offer a range of material for sorting out.

Measuring activities lead to groupings: all the children who are the same height or weight, all children who can jump the same height, all the jobs which take one minute by the 'pinger' clock, all the bottles which hold one pint. The possibilities within the classroom are endless.

This physical act of sorting produces a set. A class of objects is held together by an idea which is common to all of them. The common idea is an abstraction so that the actual criterion is an abstract idea. The classification 'long', for instance, is an idea which exists only in the mind.

Once children have had ample opportunity to talk about

their experiences and the ideas they form as a result of them, they can begin to record them on paper. Their first attempts will take the form of pictures. By representing sets of objects pictorially they are helped to see the various relationships between sets and within each set. Later they can write down their experiences in words. Only when ideas are well established will children use number symbols to represent them.

We now begin to see the complex nature of mathematical thought. The process of classification and of understanding the nature of sets is a vast accomplishment in itself. When it comes to understanding relationships, still greater intellectual activity is demanded of the child. Piaget, as we have seen, analysed thought activities in terms of operations. He associates certain properties with these systems of operations. Two of these properties are *conservation* and *reversibility*, and these principles are fundamental to mathematical reasoning.

*Conservation* means that the amount of material, as in a lump of plasticine, remains the same whatever shape it is, and that the number of objects in a group, such as a bag of sweets, remains the same however they are arranged and whether they are spread out or collected together.

*Reversibility* means that when we reverse an action we return to the original situation. These processes may seem obvious to the adult but they are by no means so to the child. Even an intelligent child must learn these principles from personal experience, and he will grasp them when his mental structures are mature enough to do so and not before.

William, aged seven, came into school one very cold morning carrying an icicle which, he confirmed, was 12 inches long. 'I shall need a one-pound jam-jar to let it melt into,' he decided. The water from the melted icicle did in fact fill the jar. William then fetched a dish. 'I bet it will just be right,' he said, and began to pour the water into the dish. William's teacher felt doubtful but made no comment while she left William to experiment. Much to her amazement, the water from the jar filled the dish exactly. Adequate opportunity to experiment in the water-corner had enabled William to develop his knowledge of conservation until it surpassed that of his teacher.

In the same classroom two boys of six and a half were playing with bricks. They had tipped the bricks from the box and when it was time to pack away the bricks were spread over a large area of floor. 'It's no good,' they said, 'we want a bigger box.' Their teacher reminded them that the bricks had fitted into the box before they started to play. The boys remained unconvinced. 'They couldn't *all* go in that box.' Persuaded by the teacher, they restored the bricks to the box. 'It's magic,' they then decided. It was some weeks later before they could accept the idea that the situation was reversible.

Incidents such as these occur daily in a classroom where children are learning through their own activities. The teacher who understands can use these spontaneous opportunities for helping the child to develop sound ideas. As adults one of our main difficulties is that we forget how we learned mathematical concepts, and we find it difficult to imagine how we should think and behave if we had not formed them. We need to discover, as Piaget did, through sharing the child's experiences how he learns to think.

We are then able to plan situations which will enlarge the meaning of the terms the child uses. Many of these situations will be natural ones, but the question arises: Is there a place for a certain amount of structured activity, for instance the use of such apparatus as that devised by Dr Dienes or Catherine Stern, and equipment such as 'Unifix'?

Structured apparatus could be seen as a bridge between the real objects of the natural situation and the abstract idea or symbol of that situation. If it is introduced at the right stage, many children can benefit from the structured situation. Adequate opportunity to experiment with real objects in their natural setting must precede the use of the contrived situation and some children can bridge the gap between the concrete situation and the abstract idea behind it unaided. The normally intelligent child might be eight or nine before he can benefit from structured material and we would be wasting his time if we introduced it sooner. It is wrong to suppose that apparatus teaches concepts and that by showing the child how to manipulate it correctly we speed the development of his ideas. What the apparatus will do is clarify and consolidate the idea the child has discovered within his everyday world of things.

Should we include the chanting of tables as a suitable mathematical activity for young children, or the verbalising of steps in mechanical arithmetic, or rote learning of number bonds? Committing tables to memory is a convenient way of carrying them around ready for use when we need them, but the feat in itself has little value and understanding of the meaning and function of tables is far more important. A lot of the teacher's skill and energy can be dissipated in such empty pursuits.

The skill of the teacher consists in devising learning situations which are rich in opportunities for discovery, and her efforts should be spent in helping the child to crystallise his ideas and to consolidate them through developing the quality of the language he uses to communicate them. When ideas and the language which expresses them are firmly established, we can turn our attention to certain useful verbal activities such as counting, to memorising tables, and to exploring the way in which numbers can be bonded together.

# 5

# Developing mathematical ideas

Keith filled a pint milk bottle with water and began to pour the contents into a little fat jug. 'It won't make it,' he said, and was very surprised when it did. Keith then collected a number of jugs and bottles. Presently he placed four of these side by side. 'They're all different shapes,' he observed, 'but they're all a pint.'

Keith went on pouring from vessel to vessel, then said to his teacher, 'The bottle gets heavy when I pour water in. Water's heavy.' His teacher asked him, 'How heavy?', and a few minutes later he replied, 'About two pounds'. 'You've weighed the *bottle* with the water,' she pointed out. Eventually Keith decided that a pint of water almost balanced the 1-lb. and the $\frac{1}{4}$-lb. weights.

From this simple experience of his physical world Keith had discovered at least two important ideas. He knew something about the permanence of material, or conservation, and he knew that water had weight and what its weight was. Adults who know less than Keith about these matters might be dismayed to hear that he spent time in school playing with water instead of doing arithmetic. As an adult, however, Keith may well develop a sounder concept of his physical world than his parents have done.

The child's ideas about substance develop as a result of the discoveries he makes about matter which he can see, feel and handle; these ideas are among the first he develops. Weight is a much more difficult idea, and ideas such as time are more difficult still.

By the time the child is two he has begun to differentiate between himself and the objects outside that self. He can recognise an apple, a wooden block, or his teddy-bear, and he knows that these objects will remain as they are even when he goes to bed. Sometimes he has milk in a cup or a lump of pastry dough in his hand. He may drink some of the milk and find there is less left in the cup. He may put two lumps of pastry together and find that this gives him more to play with. He understands something about quantity, but it is not until he is seven or eight that he will understand that the amount of any substance remains the same regardless of its shape or the rearrangements of its parts.

The child of five will roll out his lump of pastry and will tell you that there is more of it 'because it's spread out flat' Alternatively he may tell you there is less 'because it's thinner'. He depends on what he sees and when the pastry is rolled into a long sausage the lump may *look* more. If the lump is broken into small pieces which are then spread across the table, perception is deceptive and to the child there *seems* to be more.

The same problem arises whether the child is dealing with a solid mass, a collection of small objects, or a liquid. Pam, Helen and Ian, aged six, were arranging flowers for the school hall. The vase was tall and the teacher asked them, 'Which of these jugs will you need to fetch water?' All three children pointed to the large 2-pint jug and then filled it with water. Helen poured water into the vase, then looked with surprise at the jug, which was still half full. 'That was a lot too much,' she said.

Their teacher gave them a second tall vase and asked them to try again. This time water was fetched in the 1-pint jug, and this just filled the vase. Pam said, 'That was just right.'

But Ian stared at the vase and looked puzzled. 'There's more water now,' he decided. 'It's swelled. The water's swelled bigger.'

When the flowers were arranged the teacher took the children to the water-play corner. 'See if you can find bottles which you can fill from the smallest jug,' she suggested. Pam and Helen accepted that a range of containers of different shapes could be equal in capacity, but Ian remained unconvinced, and it was nearly a year later before he had grasped the idea of conservation.

Pam and Helen had also acquired some knowledge of reversibility. The teacher poured water from the pint jug into three glass jars and then asked the girls to pour the water from the jars into a second jug. When she asked how much water there was now in the second jug, she was told promptly, 'A pint'.

Experience of the physical world obviously affects the development of ideas about conservation and reversibility, but how far the acceptance of these depends on experience as opposed to age is difficult to decide. Pam and Helen and Ian had the same experiences at about the same chronological age, but Ian was not yet ready to interpret experience precisely. Many adults seem unable to grasp the idea of conservation and are easily deceived by their perceptions. Unscrupulous salesmen take advantage of this, and even intelligent adults will purchase goods sold in containers which deceive. The cone is an attractive shape and some people purchasing goods packed in a cone may not realise that a cylindrical container of the same base would contain three times the amount of the cone.

Weight is defined in the Oxford Dictionary as 'the quantity of a portion of matter as measured by the amount of its downward force due to gravity'. A child can learn about weight only through experiencing the effect objects have on his muscles, and according to Piaget a sound concept of weight develops two years later than the concept of substance.

A toddler picks up and carries an empty bucket and will try to do the same when it is full of sand, and he comes to use the terms 'light' or 'heavy' according to the effect these weights have on his muscles. He will push a little barrel up a plank and learn that he must exert considerable effort in order to get it to the top. Although he cannot express the idea in words, he is experiencing gravitational force.

The size of an object may be related to the weight of it, but often is not. Only experience will tell the child that a huge beach-ball is no heavier than a little rubber ball, and that it may be lighter than a cricket ball.

Another puzzling thing about weight is that it changes. The child watching a television programme sees the man who is as heavy as father become 'weightless' in space. Visual perception, indeed, is an unreliable guide to weight; a small glass of mercury offers a good example of this.

The child has much to learn about weight before he can understand the significance of weighing. Scales in the Nursery School are often used as part of a dramatic situation, and the Nursery baby will put his hand on the scales to make the pan go down. That is what he has seen happen when the shop man serves a customer and he is trying to reproduce the adult experience, but he isn't weighing. At this stage lifting, carrying, pushing and pulling will tell him about weight, but he isn't ready to measure it or to compare one weight with another.

The five-year-old will know that he can carry an empty box unaided but that he needs the help of a friend to carry it when it is full of soil. He enjoys blowing bubbles and can keep a bubble suspended by blowing gently. By the time he is six he will enjoy using the balance pans and making discoveries about balancing one object against another. He will discover that his bag of conkers balances a large stone from the garden. Later he will use a number of 1-oz. bags of sand or a number of ounce weights instead of stones. He may even discover by

37

experimenting that the ¼-lb. weight balances four 1-oz. weights and that the 1-lb. weight balances two ½-lb. weights, and so on. Operations such as baking and shopping will prove the need for accuracy; and the accepted fact that everybody must get the same amount of toffee for a single sixpenny bit shows him that weights must be standardised.

The idea of the conservation of weight is a later development. Experience will teach the child that the large lump of pastry weighs the same whether it is flattened out into a pancake, divided up into tart-sized pieces, or rolled out into a long thin snake. He will discover, too, that the untidy pile of bricks which overflows the box is no heavier than when neatly packed into the box, and that the huge fluffy mass of agrilon fibre weighs the same when squeezed into his tightly clenched fist. The idea of reversibility with regard to weight is slow to develop, and the child will perhaps be nine before he can grasp the idea that if his lump of pastry is broken up into small pieces, the collection of pieces will be the same weight as the original lump.

It is as the child plays and works with his materials that he begins to understand the significance of his actions, but many teachers feel unable to rely exclusively on environmental situations. There are limits to the number and variety of experiences we can set before children. It is for this reason that apparatus has been devised by people such as Cuisenaire, Dienes and Stern. Such apparatus is designed to enable the child to appreciate the significance of his own actions through rearrangement of the materials, and some attention to this kind of apparatus was given in Chapter 4. In passing it should be noted that apparatus used by Piaget was designed to examine and assess the development of a child's concepts. It was in no way designed to teach.

There is much we need yet to know about the way mathematical ideas develop in children. Controversial as the subject may be, we do now clearly recognise that many children are introduced to formal number teaching before they are intellectually ready to learn with understanding. We can teach a child to manipulate numbers dealing with the four rules in reference to pounds and ounces and we can show him how to procure the right answers, but how much this means to him depends on the quality of his experience and on the stage he has reached in the development of his mind.

In the following chapters we shall try, through our observation of the way in which children react spontaneously to their environment, to decide which kinds of situations are educative and how children working in them begin to develop mathematical and scientific ideas.

# 6

# Experiences with measurement

There is an element of measurement in almost any situation. It may relate to volume, size, capacity, height, weight, distance, time, depth, or direction, but wherever we look and whatever we do we come up against the need to compare things. In everyday life we use measurement for a purpose; we measure in order to discover how many bricks to buy, how much the curtains will cost, how far the hose-pipe must reach, or how long it will take to get home.

Some people pursue occupations which require precise measurement; most of us find approximations more useful. The concepts of measurement we carry about with us are those we use most frequently. Often proportion is of more use than exact quantity, e.g. one part fat to two of flour, or one part peat, one part leaf mould, one part sand, five parts loam for potting compost.

When working with children in school we should remember these principles. There may be brief spells when measuring is fun for its own sake, but these are fleeting. A child measures his table in order to find out how much material he needs for a table-cloth; he measures the weight of his hamster to discover the rate of its growth; he measures the height of all his friends in order to discover the average height of six-year-old boys. Measurement grows out of man's need, and this is how it should be understood. We will in this chapter consider how children begin to understand the measurement of distance, height, weight, capacity and direction.

We have seen how in the first two years of life a child develops an awareness of objects. He knows a ball and a doll, a spoon and a spade, a chair and a bed; he knows himself as a person and recognises other persons. He then begins to be aware that objects in the same class differ, and that one object can take on different forms. He uses words to discriminate between differences in amount: 'This cup is big and that one is little.' 'There was a lot of rice pudding; now there isn't much left.' 'The milk bottle is heavy.' 'The shopping basket is light when we start off.'

By the time the child enters school he is discriminating with greater precision: 'My tower is higher than John's.' 'I want a bit more string but not so much as before.'

Marie, aged five, was helping her teacher to count the biscuit money. She watched her count twelve pennies and stack them. Marie picked up a handful of pennies and began to stack them one at a time beside the teacher's pile. When the piles were level, she sat back satisfied. 'Now they're the same,' she said. 'So mine's a shilling as well.'

A crowded classroom offers some challenging mathematical situations. In order to get from one place to another without upsetting other workers means careful estimation of spaces and planning of possible routes. In one classroom the five-year-old children were annoyed when they tried to get out of the room in a huddle and found that the door would not open. One boy fetched a short jumping cane and put it on the floor at right angles to the door. 'We must stand behind that,' he said. He repeated the procedure for a day or two, forming the children into a line whenever they were leaving the room together. One day he said, 'We don't need the stick. We can guess.'

Peggy was covering a doll's house, made from a biscuit-box,

with wall-paper. In her first attempt she cut a piece from the wall-paper roll and hoped for the best. Finding it too short she added a strip. On reaching the second wall, she measured the paper against the box before cutting it.

These children had all come up against the need for measuring and were devising ways of meeting it; they were ready to be introduced to simple units which would help them.

Equipment for measuring should include rods of all lengths, string knotted at intervals, yard-sticks, tape-measures and rulers, a 'click wheel', callipers, a Gunter's chain, a surveyor's tape, dividers, and a speedometer. Capacity measures can include jars, bottles, purpose-made capacity measures, a baby's feeding-bottle, medicine bottles and cooking measures. A ship's compass and a theodolite are also interesting.

Children enjoy measuring themselves, and every aspect of measurement can be included in the experience. Besides measuring weight and height, they can measure (i) capacity, e.g. the amount of milk I drink in a week or a year; (ii) time, e.g. how many minutes it takes to get dressed, to pack away, et cetera; (iii) money, e.g. how much I spend on ice-cream in a four-week holiday; (iv) area, the area of handprints, foot-prints, and so on.

The construction of a pond in the school lawn gave rise to a great deal of purposeful linear measurement. A plan was required before the local authority would agree to the scheme, and a group of six and seven-year-old children made careful measurements before scaling them down to a paper plan. A parent brought a discarded sink to incorporate at the bottom of the pond for drainage. David, Philip and Brian measured the sink and calculated the final depth of the pond. They measured the size of the plug required, and one was then made up for them in the adjacent Secondary Boys School. Shirley and Anne calculated the length of hose required to reach the pond from the tap in the cloakroom, and then calculated the cost at a shilling per yard for the 181 feet which was purchased.

The idea of scale introduced by the plan was reinforced a week later. Brian was trying to illustrate a story about boats. He consulted the book on ships in the 'Observer' series and tried to copy the authentic models. 'They don't look right,' he complained of his own pictures. His teacher gave him some inch-squared paper, and with the aid of the statistics provided by the reference book she helped Brian to produce drawings which satisfied him.

Inspired by a piece of red satin, Susan wanted to make a top for herself. Her teacher suggested that she might like to try it in paper before cutting the satin. Susan cut her top. When she fitted it against her body she found that it was much too small. She asked for help and was shown how to use a tape-measure. 'My chest is 24 inches,' she said. 'How wide must your dress be from side to side?' asked her teacher. Susan thought for a moment and then suggested, 'About 12 inches, but it looks a lot.' She fitted a fresh top, and eventually cut and stitched her satin. She was delighted to find that the top fitted.

Marie made a purse with a button-hole. She sewed on a button, but found that it pulled when she fastened it. The teacher helped her to determine the correct position of the button.

All these children were meeting the need for measurement in everyday life, and in certain situations they realised how essential accuracy was. It is this need for accuracy, associated with units of measurement, which leads to the use of standardised measures.

The idea of comparing the weight of matter with standardised measures is introduced to children through experiments with balance pans. The four-year-old enjoys the satisfaction of making the two pans balance. His interest here is as much aesthetic as academic. Janice experimented for some time, putting an assortment of objects in both pans until the pointer indicated balance. Eventually she sorted out all the plastic cubes from a box of assorted small objects and then proceeded to select all the wooden pegs to balance against the cubes. When the pans balanced she sat back satisfied, then turned her attention to something else.

Five- and six-year-olds will use a number of identical units such as pennies, small bags filled with sand, cubes or paper-clips. When standard weights are introduced, they should include a large number of ounce weights. In this way the child can make his own discoveries about the quarter-of-a-pound weight, the pound weight, and so on.

Pennies from the shop were put into 5-shilling bags. One child said, 'They *are* heavy.' She weighed one of the bags and found that it came to 1 lb. 4 oz. 'You get sixty pennies in twenty ounces,' she declared, amazed. Later she concluded, 'If we're short of ounce weights we can use three pennies.'

Mary fetched a stone from the garden. 'It's heavy,' she said. 'It weighs 2 lb. 10 oz.' Her teacher asked, 'If it were a bigger stone could you weigh it on the scales?' Mary thought not. 'We'd have to use the weighing machine,' she said. The group then discussed the size of stones. Mary said, 'If you have a very heavy one, you wouldn't call it a stone, you'd call it a boulder.' When asked what she thought a boulder would weigh, she replied, 'Tons and tons.'

Experience of heavy weight is comparatively rare, but examples do arise. Children weigh themselves and can record their weight and the weight of others; the arrival of coke for the school boiler gives them a chance to see what a ton of coke looks like; coal may be delivered to their homes in 1-cwt. bags; and they may sometimes help mother to carry home a stone of potatoes. Sand and clay for use in school are often packed in 14- and 28-lb. bags, so children can try lifting a stone or half-stone weight.

In one school a strong wooden pulley was fixed to a beam in the corridor and a bucket attached to the end of a rope which passed over it. House bricks were weighed and placed in the bucket, and the children experimented to find out how much more they could lift with the aid of the pulley. They thus began to understand an important principle of machinery.

Children heard the story of David and Goliath, and the word 'cubit' was explained to them. Two boys marked off a length of string with knots and measured out six cubits on the playground. 'Goliath was only as big as a man,' they exclaimed in disgust. The teacher reminded them that they had used their own forearms for cubits and that they should use a man's instead. The boys made a fresh start, knotting the string in lengths of a man's cubit. They then drew a giant six cubits long and a boy of three cubits beside him. 'He was *really* big,' they decided.

Through the classroom window two boys from the neighbouring Secondary Boys School were seen on the games-field. They were using a surveyor's chain and a theodolite. A group of boys from the Infant School went over and were told they were making a survey of the school site. The young boys were shown the chain, and they counted its one hundred links; two of them sited points through the theodolite, and noticed the compass indicating direction.

The following day their teacher brought a mine surveyor's theodolite and added it to a collection of measuring equipment. Some of the boys brought pocket compasses and made various discoveries, as that 'the head-mistress's room is north-east of our classroom'. The compasses were also found to be useful in their observation of the weather. N, S, E and W were marked out on the playground, and a simple wind flag was erected to ascertain the direction of the wind.

One boy brought a news cutting about sun spots. He smoked some glass to observe them and this led to an interest in the sun's course. Thus the interest in measuring direction was also extended.

Mathematical instruments are in themselves a source of exploration. Precision is aesthetically pleasing, and an instru-

45

ment such as a micrometer can be explored with the help of the teacher. One group of children measured the thickness of their hair and were very surprised to find that it varied considerably.

One foggy day, a group of children measured the distance walked by one boy before he disappeared into the fog. It came to about 25 yards. Their teacher told them that they had measured the visibility, thus introducing another dimension of radio weather-forecasts.

Discovery of mathematical ideas at this stage ranges over many types of measurement and is largely a matter of making comparisons. Children are grasping the main concepts of measurement, and, as their thought processes mature, these ideas become more highly organised.

# 7

# Experiences with time

Time is one of the most difficult concepts to grasp and it means very little to the young child. Experience of time *takes* time and a small child hasn't lived long enough to know what time means. Because of its abstract nature few adults develop a really sound time sense. What we know about time does not prevent us from assessing it according to what we are doing; interest and boredom can be very misleading. Faced with the question as to what time is we should be at a loss to explain.

> Time present and time past
> Are both perhaps present in time future,
> And time future contained in time past.
>
> T. S. Eliot. *Burnt Norton.*

When drawing, a small child will represent a number of time sequences in the same picture; he may draw himself having his breakfast, going to school and being at school. He is not aware of the different times in which events have occurred, and is more concerned with presenting action which involves him.

By the time he is three a child can beat out a rhythm on a drum, he uses words such as 'day' and 'night', 'bath-time' and 'tea-time', but his concept of time remains quite undeveloped.

The four-year-old begins to recognise sequence. He knows that dinner-time follows breakfast-time and that the next meal after dinner will be tea. He begins to use the words 'today', 'yesterday' and 'tomorrow', and will remember that Christmas-time comes after holiday-time and that his birthday comes in between.

The child of five sees his day as an unbroken piece of time in which events flow on from one to another. His rhythm patterns are uneven and individual to him. He has difficulty in trying to move to the disciplined rhythm of a piece of music or to a rhythm beaten out by the teacher.

He associates certain actions with certain times in the day. If he is asked to put on his coat in order to go on to the playground, he may think it is time to go home for dinner, although he has been in school for barely half an hour. When the six- or seven-year-old talks about 'ancient times', he may mean when grandmother was a little girl or he may mean in the days of cave-men.

Time is fundamental to science, and teachers feel the need to help children understand time as a highly significant concept in our scientific age. Time controls our lives and is essential to life in our complex culture. If all clocks and watches were to stop, the effect would be a complete breakdown of life as we know it. When a child starts coming to school the rigidity of man's adopted time-pattern is imposed on him.

The fact that a child can 'tell the time' may mean simply that he can read the dial of the clock and describe the position of the fingers on it, and he may be able to do this without having any idea what these symbols represent. We must, however, help him to do this if only for social purposes.

One inexpensive alarm-clock can be far more use to the children than a dozen wooden or cardboard clocks. A 'pinger' clock, a stop-watch, a pendulum, a metronome, egg-timer, hourglass, sundial, equipment to make a water-clock or a candle-clock, calendars and time-tables and time-sheets are all helpful pieces of equipment.

Children can gain a concept of time passing by seeing a physical change take place as a result of time. Jam tarts go into the oven and after 15 minutes have undergone a spectacular change. Given time, sugar dissolves, cloth is dyed, photographic paper prints, peas and children grow. In such operations time is an essential feature, and the introduction of precision is important.

A seven-year-old using a 'pinger' clock made the following observations:

'It takes me five minutes to write fourteen lines of a story.' 'It takes half a minute to tie my shoe laces.' 'We can pack away in two minutes.' 'It takes four minutes to put out the P. E. apparatus.'

We complicate things by measuring time in a number of different ways:

A year is the measure of the earth's journey round the sun.

A lunar month is the measure of the moon's journey round the earth.

A day is the measure of time between sunrise and sunrise, or the rotation of the earth on its axis.

A week is a religious division of time and a year is divided into twelve months which have little to do with the moon.

Much of what we have said so far is concerned with helping the child to fit into the framework of modern society. But underlying the order of the universe is a time-pattern which is closer to the child's understanding and which reaches him in the form of rhythm.

A child's experience of rhythm starts before he is born. The sensation of his mother's heart-beats and of her blood coursing rhythmically through his body are the child's introduction to the rhythm of life. The rhythm of his own body, of night and day, of the seasons, of the recurrence of Christmas and holidays impinges on the child and by the time he is four he will know that 'he will have another birthday next year'.

The clock is a mechanical device which treats time as sequence; it is the only way we know of synchronising the practical business of daily life. We grow to think of time as ticked away by the clock, but life itself is measured by rhythm and natural rhythm treats life as a cycle without beginning and without end. Sequence acquires new meaning in this concept and rhythmic continuity takes precedence.

At the age of fifteen months Julie would bang with her spoon on her tray. The pattern was uneven and the rhythm immature. A month later she enjoyed 'This little pig went to market' and other forms of toe and finger play, and her favourite game was 'Dance-a-baby-didee', accompanied by rhythmic bouncing on a parent's knee. When seated in Grandma's rocking-chair she would rock to and fro for hours.

Swings remain the most popular pieces of play apparatus on the children's play-park. The child in the Infant and Nursery School loves the story which depends on repetition. Rhythmic patterns of sound produced by percussion instruments are favourite forms of music-making in the Infant School, and a child will respond more readily in dance to rhythm tapped out with percussion instruments than he will to melody. Indeed, for quite a long time he remains more aware of rhythm than melody in music and may be quite unable to respond to imposed rhythm at all. The young child has an individual and unformed rhythm of his own which rarely corresponds to the rhythm dictated by a tune. Very often music played for a child to dance or sing to remains meaningless and in fact simply goes on while he moves or chants to his own rhythm.

The child's love and appreciation of rhythm become evident in his picture-making and in the patterns he designs in clay and other media. As he masters language he begins to appreciate the rhythmic use of words in prose and poetry. He may try himself to create form from words.

Sheila, aged seven, was intensely interested in weather

phenomena and kept records of weather observations with great care. In one book she recorded the seasons in pictures and wrote appropriate comments for each season of the year. About autumn she wrote:

'It is autumn and all the leaves are turning different colours and all the fruit has grown on the trees. The clouds are sirus and stratus. The leaves are off the trees in all patterns of different colours and waves. It makes all patterns the wind does with the leaves. Everywhere is pretty on the ground. The frost will soon be here. The birds are flying away. Only the Robins are with us. We are collecting wood for winter. There are not many flowers now.'

The rhythm and balance of her sentences matched her theme.

So basic is rhythm to life that any attempt to disturb it evokes dramatic attempts to regain it. The homeostasis of the human body (see Chapter 15) is a good example. Loss of sight is compensated by increased sensitivity in touch and hearing. The locust which loses a leg makes haste to grow another. Weeds struggling in thick undergrowth grow tall to reach the sun.

Rhythm is not confined to living things. The small child experiences the bouncing of a ball and the rhythmic beating of waves on the beach. A six-year-old child will watch in fascination the swing of a pendulum or the perpetual spinning of a top.

Early man lived close to the order of things. When he began to organise his day he based his devices on natural rhythm provided by the sun, or the rhythm of water leaking through a hole or of sand falling evenly through an aperture. These early modes of telling the time interest six- to seven-year-old children. Richard wrote a book called 'Time through the Ages', and these are some of the entries:

'Long ago for telling the time they used sand and sun and water . . . If you put a stick in the ground on a sunny day the stick throws a shadow on the ground. At different times in the day the shadow will be in a different place . . . The Egyptians got a stone bowl and put a hole in the bottom and measured out twelve hours. The water would leak out and when the water reached the bottom 12 hours had gone . . . An egg-timer lasts about 3 minutes. Some sand-timers are meant for special purposes and last an hour. . .'

David, aged six, was interested in Big Ben. 'We live in England,' he wrote. 'Big Ben tells us the time. When Big Ben has stopped there would be no check-up.'

On another occasion the introduction of a globe into the classroom provoked his curiosity. He wanted to know what 'those lines' (the longitude lines) were for. This is what he made of his teacher's explanation: '15 degrees East and West makes 1 hour difference. So if it is 4 o'clock here it will be 5 o'clock there.'

When a child understands something about time passing and the way in which the clock denotes sequence he becomes interested in imposing pattern on his day-to-day experiences. Ann wrote about breakfast-time: 'I have my breakfast at 8.15. My friend Patricia has her breakfast at 7.30 as her mother goes to work at 8.30. It takes four minutes to boil a soft egg, ten minutes to boil a hard egg and five minutes to cook bacon.'

Stewart, a keen footballer, wrote: 'If I went to see Wolves at home I would go to Midland Station and catch the 7.30 train to Birmingham. It would take 1½ hours, that would be 9 o'clock. From Birmingham to Wolverhampton is about half an hour. I would walk round the town for a half hour till 10 o'clock then go to a cafe or fish and chip shop for my lunch, for a quarter of an hour. And then go to find the ground. Then it would be 10.15. If you want a good view wait out till 12 o'clock then I would have some sandwiches. I would buy a cup of tea and then buy a programme. They would let you in the ground an hour before the kick-off that would be 2 o'clock if the kick-off was 3 o'clock.'

Old clocks and watches are at all stages a source of enthusiastic investigation, and some of the popular watch manufacturers publish excellent illustrated booklets showing the parts of a watch and how a watch works. The investigation of clockwork is considered along with other mechanical principles in Chapter 16.

# 8

# Experiences with shape

By the time a baby is twelve months old he is beginning to recognise his mother as a person apart from himself. With the aid of his hands and his eyes he has found the various parts of his body, where *he* ends and things outside himself begin. His body is composed of a number of shapes. He moves in space and his body takes up space. His clothes have recognisable shapes, and these shapes change in appearance according to whether they are ironed out flat or whether he is inside them. He may be a small shape in a big space, but he grows increasingly aware of himself as a separate and independent shape. The map of his own body is beginning to take shape in his mind.

At all stages, shape is very meaningful to the young child. He uses many shapes, such as mug, drum and spoon, to which he gives names. He begins to draw and tries to represent three-dimensional shapes on flat paper. He manipulates clay, turning the same piece into a lump, a flat pancake or a long snake. He discovers that dry sand pours into a cone, that water takes the shape of the vessel he pours it into, and that from the piece of pastry his mother gives him he can cut a number of shapes which can all be the same or each one different.

He also runs round and round in circles; he bounces a ball; he traces the spiral of a snail's shell with his finger; he uses tools which have shapes to suit their purpose – a hammer, a pair of scissors, a spade, and so on – and he builds towers, bridges and ramps and digs ditches and moats. All these experiences help the child to realise that each shape has a purpose and function, that shapes define spaces, and that the various parts of space are related.

Shape incorporates mathematical discipline: there are regular two-dimensional shapes such as triangles, rectangles, squares, diamonds and parallelograms; and there are regular solid shapes, such as cones, cubes, pyramids, spheres and cylinders. Irregular shapes can be two- or three-dimensional, and the young child's first study of shapes in school should begin with solid, irregular shapes, as these are the ones with which he is most familiar and which already mean something to him.

One way of initiating an interest in shape is by collecting various articles and by encouraging the children to bring shapes they enjoy, to form a display. A discussion of these and their purpose soon indicates the fact that shapes fall into two groups: natural and man-made.

Nature produces a great variety of shapes. For instance, the snail, the crab and the oyster each has an individually shaped shell, the one that is best suited to its own habits and environment.

From a display of shells a group of children selected the snail shells as being the most exciting. They traced the 'spiral' of the design with their fingers. The word 'coil' was introduced, and the children associated it with the spring in a sofa, the big spring in a mechanical toy and the spring in a watch.

Later, in a 'movement' lesson, the children made coiled shapes. They then started collecting pictures for a 'Shape Book'. In this were represented bridges of all kinds, aerial views of a town, faces and other parts of the body, utensils and tools, vehicles, shells, songs and poems, houses, an igloo, flower arrangements, furniture, a game of chess and a military tattoo.

Crystals are also interesting natural shapes. Crystals formed from any single substance are similar in shape, but different substances form their own characteristically shaped crystals.

Hills and valleys are the natural results of the effects of weather on different types of rocks. Water takes different natural forms, such as ripples, waves, fountains and cascades. The wind blows sand into dunes, and the sea spreads the sand along the shore, sometimes leaving it in ridges. The bodies of animals and of man are shaped for the natural functions they need to perform.

With the aid of pictures cut from magazines and of illustrations of their own making, some five-year-old children compiled the following simple books on shape: 'Catherine's book of shapes', which included eggs, bowls, cubes, trees, a snake, a spire, and an urn; 'Old shapes and new shapes', involving aeroplanes, cars, boats, tables, churches and clothing; and 'A book of cloud shapes'.

Man's first tool was a stone. A hard stone with a sharp edge provided him with a weapon and, later, with an axe. Since then he has designed an infinite variety of tools and instruments shaped to meet his needs.

Kitchen utensils and furniture are designed to fulfil special functions; musical instruments and vehicles also have functional shapes. Wheels and propellers, pistons and windmills are designed to transmit power. Poems and songs make a shape on the page of a book. Cardboard containers are very cleverly designed, and opening them out shows how they were planned in the flat.

Two children supported a plank with two boxes, and three boys were able to stand on the 'bridge'. A child of four managed to haul a bucket, heavy with bricks, high above his head, by running a rope tied to the bucket over the rung of a climbing frame. Another boy prised a marble out of a hole with a ruler. In each case the child was exploring a mathematical principle. Principles such as these determine the design of the tools man makes.

Children are fascinated by bridges and most of them travel enough nowadays to see a variety of principles employed in their design. Bridges are designed to span and to carry a load, and their construction is governed by the shaping of the material used and the way in which the weight is distributed. A piece of rope will not support a weight at its top, but will support the same weight hung from it; a piece of paper will not support a weight on one edge, but will when coiled into a cylindrical shape.

Simple bridges are made of planks and rope. The Roman aqueduct consisted of three tiers of small arches, as a single tier would have collapsed under its own weight. In the cantilever bridge, each arm is balanced on a support or pier which is joined to the next so that the load is distributed. In the suspension bridge, the frame is suspended from an inverted arch.

The movement of a compass or a pendulum traces a restricted shape, but a top spins in a changing pattern of movement. A conker tied to the end of a piece of string whirls in circles, and when we stir tea, saw wood, hammer nails or comb hair, we trace other patterns of movement.

A group of children who were particularly interested compiled a 'Book of Movement'. The first pictures they selected were of water cascading and foaming as it left a lake and became confined to the river. They discussed the movement of water and used the following words: 'swirling', 'floating', 'drifting', 'sinking', 'flowing', 'rushing', 'gushing'. Other pictures were of clouds, hands, people and animals moving in various ways.

Every journey to school makes a shape. At the end of the street we turn a corner: this is an angle. The road followed during a holiday traces an interesting shape across the map. Several children, using pencils of different colours, traced the shape of their journey to school on a plan of their housing estate drawn out by the teacher. Two of the children made independent picture maps of 'what I saw on the way to school'.

Some things retain their shape while they change in size; we can buy cups, basins and measures in graded sizes. Soap in the bath retains its shape but grows smaller, while the inflation of a balloon illustrates the reverse process. Photographs are small sizes of the shapes they represent; a child grows in size but remains much the same shape.

Roger made a book called 'Shapes that grow bigger or smaller'. One of the pages was devoted to the telescope, and he was reasoning as he wrote:

'The telescope makes things come nearer. If you saw something far away and you wanted to see what it was, look through a telescope and it will come nearer so that you can see what it is. The telescope doesn't make the things come nearer but makes them look bigger.'

Chinese characters on a birthday card interested one child. When she was told that this was writing, she wanted to know what it said. She then wanted to know what numbers looked like in Chinese and tried to reproduce the characters which were found for her in a reference book.

Another child made a clay bowl. She decorated the rim with hieroglyphics, similar to those she had seen in the same book. 'That's Egyptian picture writing,' the teacher told her. 'I wonder what it says?' She took the child with her bowl to the local library to see whether the librarian could help. The librarian ordered a reference book for the purpose, and it was eventually decided that the pictures represented a prayer to the god Thoth.

A picture of the Pyramids in a reference book attracted the attention of other children in the group. Illustrations showing how they were constructed absorbed these children, and later they made a book of shapes in which they recorded:

'A pyramid has four sides. The Egyptians built the Pyramids in the deserts of Egypt. The Egyptians used cubes of stone on the ground and the first stones were laid in a square. Another smaller square of stones was laid on top of it. And another smaller on top of that. And gradually it got high until it is a point.'

This interest in shape encouraged the children to write more books than did any other interest, probably because its tangible nature made recording simple.

A book called 'Shapes in the kitchen' included bowls, cake tins, cutlery, crockery and electrical gadgets.

'Shapes in the sky' contained pictures of clouds, the sun and the planets, the moon in its changing shapes, lightning and tornadoes, hail and snow blizzards, and a rainbow.

'Shapes of birds and animals' included a swan, a lizard, a shark, an elephant, bird beaks and feet, and birds' eggs.

A book of 'Round shapes' illustrated a plate, money, buttons, wheels, lids, a tray, a gong, a drum, a tambourine, picture frames and a mirror.

Another book was about balls of all kinds. This included cricket balls, footballs, a rubber ball, woolly balls, a fireball, and a beach ball.

Graham, aged six, made a delightful book entitled 'Why is it that shape?' Some of his entries ran as follows:

'A ship has a pointed front to cut through the water.

Marbles are round so that they roll in the game.

Cats' ears are shaped like this so that they catch the sound of mice at night.

The nose of an aeroplane cuts through the air quickly. The wings keep it gliding on the air.

The river is curly because the water runs down the mountain to the sea.'

A general interest in shape also developed when a group of children were making a 'Book of Materials'. Samples of different fabrics were brought by the children from home. As they pasted them in the book they chattered: 'This piece looks like a fish', 'This is a triangle-shaped piece', and so on.

The teacher encouraged them to talk about the shapes they knew.

During the winter, when the ground beyond the classroom window was covered with snow, one child noticed the bird-tracks and footprints in the snow, and the teacher showed the children the shapes of snow crystals. Some of the words used by the children during subsequent discussion, e.g. 'twisted', 'spiral', 'craggy', were used by the teacher to suggest movements in the 'movement' lesson. Later, some of the children made a book which they called 'We make shapes as we move'. Others made books of shape words.

Shape seems to come very near to the child. It concerns him and his relationships with things and with people, the way he moves and the way in which he can manipulate his environment. Not only is it easily observable, but it forces itself to his attention in every aspect of his living. His discovery of shape, its function and purpose, involves the child in all he grows to understand of the world.

# 9

# Finding out about soil and living things

In the narrow street flanked by terraced houses not a single green growing thing was to be seen. The only glimpse of beauty was a thin strip of sky pierced by television aerials and chimney pots. Life overflowed from cluttered homes, and refuse mouldered in the gutter.

At the top of a flight of stone steps sat a little girl about $2\frac{1}{2}$ years old. On a sheet of newspaper in front of her was spread a mound of damp soil. The child scrabbled in it gleefully and at that moment her whole world consisted of the damp smell and the crumbling earth in her fingers. Her innate need to explore the stuff of the world had been satisfied by an imaginative adult.

In an Infant School classroom a group of five-year-old children shared a similar experience. Their teacher had provided a mound of damp soil and lumps of turf. One boy was fascinated by the way grass roots bound the soil into clumps, and he hacked at the turf with an old table-knife. The girl at his side found a worm. She placed it on a sheet of paper and listened as it scratched its way across. With the aid of a reading glass she examined it carefully. She then peered amongst the soil through the glass, poking from time to time but making no comment. Her questions would arise when she began to understand; for the moment to be lost in discovery was enough.

'Among the mind's powers is one that comes of itself to many children and artists. It need not be lost, to the end of his days, by anyone who has ever had it. This is the power of taking delight in a thing, or rather, in anything . . . A child in the full health of his mind will put his hand flat on the summer turf, feel it, and give a little shiver of private glee at the elastic firmness of the globe' (C. E. Montague, *Disenchantment*, 1922).

Children have a deep appreciation of natural objects, or, as they often call them, 'real things'. They possess an infinite capacity for becoming lost in whatever catches their interest. For them there is no such thing as not having time to stare. Lacking conscious awareness of time makes infinity possible and what absorbs them constitutes the whole of their world.

Teachers have always acknowledged this and from the earliest days of the Infant School a 'nature table' has been given an honoured position. Unfortunately adults tend to lose the child's sense of wonder and sometimes nature tables become ossified and the miscellany of twigs, seeds, flowers and fruits, usually labelled, becomes a familiar part of the landscape and eventually deteriorates into a morgue.

If we have things living and growing in the classroom, they should do so vigorously and naturally. The eternal pea snuggling beside a piece of pink blotting paper tells the child what it can in its first message. He doesn't need a repeat performance every few weeks.

We could interpret the term nature table as meaning any investigation table intended to direct the child's attention to observation of his natural world. The diversity of material we can put there is as wide as the world itself.

One such table presented the varied contents of a hedge-bottom. The collection contained leaves and leaf mould, the skeleton of a dead leaf, some pieces of straw, a feather, a scrap of wool from a sheep's back, pieces of bark, spiders, harvesters, wood-lice, hawthorn twigs with buds on the point of opening, fresh blades of grass springing from a lump of rotting wood, and some fronds of dead bracken.

The following week on the same table children observed a selection of objects found in the soil. There were fossils, rocks, pebbles, sand, lumps of chalk, chunks of iron pyrites and crystalline silica, marble, alabaster: a whole range of materials which form the crust of the earth.

Some of the children experimented with the soil itself. They collected empty yoghurt containers and grew seeds under a variety of conditions – with and without light, water, soil, et cetera. They came to some conclusions about the essentials of growth.

On another occasion objects from the seashore occupied the nature table. Shells, driftwood, skeletons and sponges, sand, pebbles, a sea-urchin and various kinds of dried sea-weed were displayed. A wide range of interests stemmed from this display embracing the bed of the ocean, deep-sea diving, lobster and oyster fishing, sand-dunes and coastal protection, as well as the more obvious interests in shipping and fishing and ocean voyages.

One group of seven-year-old children collected all sorts of things 'About Trees'. They set out pieces of bark from elm, beech, willow and oak trees, beechmast, conkers, acorns, sycamore and ash wings, dead leaves and a set of photographs showing the same lime tree at different times of the year. This led to an extensive investigation of the many uses of wood, and objects ranging from wooden spoons and stools to paper and cardboard were displayed. The uses of wood 'in bygone days' and of 'wood in other parts of the world' were included in this interest.

Do we have animals living in the classroom? In one school hamsters and mice are kept in a well-lit and ventilated storeroom. The children are responsible for their care and take them home at holiday times. Records are kept of the weight and growth of these pets. The children watch them breed and can tell a visitor why their coats are marked as they are.

In some schools hens are reared and careful accounts of the eggs produced and sold provide realistic exercises in arithmetic. There are a few schools which go so far as to keep pigs, even a cow or a donkey. In many schools rabbits are free to range about the classrooms. Here and there we find schools which maintain a pet corner apart from the classrooms.

An aquarium has a wide appeal. It is not easy to establish the correct balance of life in one and a teacher approaching the venture for the first time should seek advice from an aquarium shop and follow the instructions published in a reputable book on the subject. Fish kept in a bowl rarely survive. March each year brings bowls and buckets of tadpoles. What we do about these things must depend on individual enthusiasm, for only the teacher who is an enthusiast will succeed in creating vital learning situations along these lines.

A vivarium is more easily maintained, and in many ways much more exciting, for few children can resist the attraction of insects or worms and there are plenty to find in almost any habitat. Equipment costs next to nothing; a strong box filled with rubbish from the hedge-bottom will house insects and a large glass sweet-jar filled with damp soil provides a home for worms.

The intensity of a child's interest in living things makes him an extremely active learner and material of this kind appeals even to children who are normally less responsive to the school situation.

Judith wasn't an intellectually gifted child and many experiences failed to stir her. A vivarium was established in the classroom and Judith's interest was caught. She was particularly attracted by the caterpillars; she really seemed to love these furry creatures and kept them in a glass jam-jar which she took with her wherever she went. One day she settled at the writing-table with her jar of caterpillars in front of her, and made her first book of pictures about the way they crawled.

Carboy gardens are quite easy to set up and are highly suitable for indoor cultivation. Children have an advantage over adults when planting them as their small hands squeeze easily through the aperture. A shallow layer of path chippings with a layer of compost on top will serve to anchor moss, small ferns, Tradescantia and miniature London Pride. Watered and sealed, these little gardens will continue to grow without further attention. Here we have a complete little world living on itself in a sealed jar, and the child peering through the glass into the quiet green fronds is lost in the sheer wonder of what he sees.

The use of a reading glass or a microscope adds another dimension to observation. With the help of the teacher children can learn to appreciate the exquisite delicacy of the fabric which composes living things. The use of these aids will be referred to from time to time in chapters on other aspects of discovery.

Soil is one of the child's most natural playthings, and making mud pies is a most absorbing occupation. The crust of the earth and the living things which depend on it are basic materials to learning, and children should be provided with ample opportunity to pursue their inborn interest in them.

# 10

# Finding out about water

Exploration of the environment could very well start with water, for water is essential to life and does in fact make up the largest part of any living tissue. Even the youngest child is brought into contact with water every day. It is easy to observe water. We can feel it, see it, and hear it. Much is learned about it merely by watching its behaviour.

The child's experience of water may be said to start before birth. For nine months the child exists in the soothing security of a warm sea; and, although we know little about the child's impressions at this stage, the attraction that water holds for people of all ages may stem from before birth. In adult life, water in all its moods continues to captivate us, and the therapeutic effect of water is widely recognised.

After birth, the child has frequent contact with water. He will splash in his bath; he will drink water; as he grows older he will paddle in it, swim in it, play with it and see it being used by others in a great many ways. One of his joys on entering school is a plumbing system scaled down so that he can operate it unaided. By this time he will be fairly familiar with reflections, ripples and waves, rain and snow, fountains, lakes and rivers. When allowed, he will spend hours of complete absorption at the kitchen sink, where the mere presence of water assures his avid interest.

With some guidance from the teacher, the child's experiments can become more systematic, and his discoveries can be clarified and deepened.

We can start by providing equipment which will enable the child to discover the properties and behaviour of water: bottles, jars, jugs and tins of all shapes and sizes, a set graded in size (e.g. 'Marmite' jars), 'squeeze' bottles, rubber and transparent tubing, a hose with jet and sprinkler attachment, funnels and sieves, things which float or sink, liquid measures, a pump, a sponge, a bucket, and simple materials and chemicals such as salt, sugar, and permanganate of potash.

Where there is no running water in the classroom, a large container, such as a zinc bath or water trolley, is essential; this can be filled from the cloakroom tap with the aid of a hose. Empty five-gallon polythene sherry containers can also provide a source of running water in any classroom. One school even constructed its own pond (see Chapter 6), using an old sink for drainage and lining the sides with concrete.

A good supply of reference books should also be made available so that teachers and children can further their discoveries together.

An obvious property of water is that it is wet. Children know from the effects of rain on their clothes that some substances are absorbent and some are not, and that the nylon dress dries quickly whereas the cloth cap takes a long time.

A group of children soaked a variety of fabrics, such as nylon, cotton, silk, rexine, velvet and wool. They stretched them to dry on the radiator and recorded the time taken. They discovered that nylon dried in nine minutes and wool in one hour, and that the remainder ranged between these two extremities. They repeated this experiment under differing conditions; for instance, some material was crushed into a ball, some put in a cold place, some hung on a line on a windy day, and so on.

67

They then asked why macintoshes kept out the rain, and how tents and umbrellas kept people dry. With the help of a reference book the teacher showed the children how to experiment with material stretched over a basin, varying the degree of tautness. Later she asked them why soap was used when washing, and together she and the children discovered information which the children interpreted as: 'Soap and detergents make it easier for the water to make things wet.'

Things dissolve in water. Some children noticed that in hot water 'things dissolve better'; a solution of sugar and water was left to cool and evaporate and the children found that something was left. Another time, a sugar solution was heated over a candle for about twenty minutes and only caramel 'toffee' was left.

During this experiment one child, carrying a jug of water from the cloakroom tap, said, 'The jug's heavy to carry when it's full of water.' This offered the teacher an opportunity for helping the children to discover the weight of water – that 'one pint weighs nearly 20 ounces'.

'A camel's hump must be heavy,' one boy remarked. Later he observed thoughtfully, 'Only camels could live on the moon, because they could drink a lot of water and carry it in their humps for a very long time.'

The weather turned cold. 'We've found a lot of ice on top of the bird-bath,' the children reported. 'The water we put in last night has turned to ice.'

'Is it frozen to the bottom?' the teacher asked. The children returned to investigate.

'No,' they reported. 'It's only at the top. It's frozen at the top first.'

They collected the blocks of ice in a bowl and thrust the thermometer amongst them. With breathless excitement they watched the temperature drop until the thermometer stood at 38 degrees. One child pointed to the thermometer reading. 'It should go down to 32 degrees,' he noted.

When the snow came the children recorded the time taken at different temperatures for a jam-jar full of snow to melt. They discovered that melting-time in a hot place was a quarter of an hour, in a warm place three-quarters of an hour, and in a cold place four hours.

Water will turn to steam. When children breathe on the window pane in cold weather the windows get steamed up. The kettle boils: there seems to be a gap between the spout and the cloud of steam; when the steam comes into contact with a cool wall, it starts to trickle down in rivulets. The use of steam in railway locomotives fascinates most children – perhaps some child will receive as a present a model steam engine with a solid-fuel heater.

Water will pour; pouring from one vessel to another is an absorbing occupation at a very early age. It is found that water takes the shape of the vessel which contains it. For instance, one measure of water will fill containers of various shapes and will fill the space completely, for it will push out the air.

Water is heavier than air and will only pour downwards. Tins of equal size can be pierced with one, two or three holes in the base. 'Does the tin with two holes empty in half the time taken by the tin with one hole?' A vertical row of holes also has an interesting effect on water pouring out of tins. A tin with a tight-fitting lid pierced at the top and bottom makes a simple valve. Children can also investigate the question: 'Why do we have to pierce the orange-juice tin twice before the juice will pour out?'

Children know what happens to flowers and plants when they have no water. Two children experimented with vegetables to see whether they contained water too. When a potato weighing 5 oz. was roasted and weighed again, it had lost 1 oz. Then a raw carrot, weighing 1½ oz., was exposed to the warm air of the classroom for two days; it shrivelled and only weighed ½ oz. Two brussels sprouts weighed ½ oz.; two days later they had shrivelled and only balanced one farthing.

One day a boy of six and a half baked some bread. He weighed and kneaded his materials, and, with the help of the teacher, the bread was baked in the oven. The cooling loaves were covered with a cloth, and one little girl noticed steam rising from under the cloth. 'Why did we mix in water if it all comes off again?' she asked. The teacher asked her to try making bread without water. A discussion followed, and the children realised that water held the materials together. They then discussed the use of water as a binding agent when cooking and when mixing paste. 'Do you think there is any water left in the bread we eat?' asked the teacher. The children thought not. Some pieces of bread from a wrapped loaf were put in a screw-top glass jar and placed on the radiator. After 20 minutes moisture appeared on the side of the glass jar. The jar was then forgotten until a fortnight later when, thanks to a negligent caretaker, it was found behind the hot pipes. The bread was covered with mould. The children were thrilled with their 'little green plants'. When asked what the mould was living on, one child suggested 'vitamins'. They then considered the ingredients and decided that the water which had evaporated from the bread and the heat from the hot pipes were responsible for this complete little world living inside a screw-top glass jar.

A microscope was then borrowed from the headmistress's room, and threads from the mould were examined. It was a dull day, so the children illuminated the microscope with a bicycle lamp. By the end of the afternoon all the children in the school were queueing up to see the little green heads with the spores popping out.

In pre-school days it is sufficiently interesting to pull the chain in the toilet and watch the miracle happen; but the school-age child wants to know where the water comes from and where it goes to: 'Why can we get hot or cold water out of taps?' 'How does the hot water get into the radiator?' And even when children know some of the answers they want to go further. 'But where does all the water in the river and the reservoir come from?' And when they are told about the rain they want to know: 'What makes it rain?'

Floods in one area focused the attention of the children on the weather. They brought photographs from the local newspaper and recorded that the boiler-room of the school was flooded. Their observation of the weather continued and the thermometer and barometer were read daily; they also made a simple wind anemometer. Their daily records read like this: 'Thursday, February 4th. Thermometer 46 degrees. Barometer 29·6 degrees. Wind W. The little man is out for rain. The wind anemometer went round 16 times in one minute. That is 7 mph.'

Later they began to notice a relationship between the barometer reading and the weather: 'The umbrella lady is out and the air pressure is low.'

In anticipation of a school outing to a zoo some fifty miles away, a group of seven-year-old children rang the local weather station and talked to the weather man. This event sparked off an interest in the work of the duty forecaster, and an illustrated article in a local paper helped with pictures and information. The children compiled a 'Weather Book' which started with the explanation 'Water goes round and round'. The accompanying illustrations indicated their dawning concept of the weather cycle.

Children visiting the seaside know something about the tides. Children who live in rural areas are naturally close to the rhythm of nature – to the river in all its moods and to the need for irrigation. Young television viewers are familiar with bathyscopes, submarines and deep-sea divers, and a discussion with a discerning adult can help children to clarify and organise much of the desultory information which reaches them.

One school acquired a large globe. At first the interest was in spinning it round, but a group of children very soon became interested in the patterns on it, and a surprising amount of latent knowledge was drawn out of them.

David collected a number of facts and made a book which he called 'My World Book'. One of the ideas which appealed to him most was the amount of blue, representing sea. 'It's nearly *all* sea,' he observed. Later he made this entry in his book:

'The large stretches of sea is called the oceans. There are 4 oceans. There are pacific oceans, atlantic oceans, indian oceans, arctic oceans. The pacific ocean is the biggest. Seven parts water and three parts land. It is 25,000 miles all round.'

Some reference has been made to the records kept by children and to the need to help them to record their observations systematically. Many children in the Infant School are limited in their ability to record on paper, and if a child is pressed to keep elaborate records too soon much of the joy of discovery is lost.

The first records made by children are verbal. Something exciting happens, so they want to talk about it and usually they tell their teacher. In the early stages the teacher can be the child's tool. Many of the incidents recorded in these books were written down by teachers, and books for such entries were kept in the headmistress's room. When a significant event occurred a teacher would fetch the book and enter it, or else send it written on a piece of paper for the headmistress to enter. Sometimes a child would make the report verbally, and in a few cases the child would write up the incident. Books made by children are also a valuable part of a school's records, and the contents of such books are quoted frequently throughout this series.

An extremely valuable aspect of this work is the collecting of words. Water coming out of a tap is described as 'gushing', 'flowing', 'dripping', 'dribbling' or 'squirting'; one of these words naturally comes nearer than the others to being an accurate description of the water's behaviour. Sometimes the words themselves are sheer fun: 'splutter', 'gurgle', 'deluge', 'soak', 'seep', 'drench', 'humid', 'muggy', 'damp'. Or they can be simply 'Our new words', e.g. 'evaporate', 'cascade', 'immerse', 'saturated', 'buoyant'.

A child may catch the idea behind a new word rather than its exact meaning. One six-year-old boy, coming into school after a strenuous P.E. lesson, puffed, 'Ooh! I bet I've lost pints with evaporation.' Such incidents provide excellent opportunities for the teacher to help the child to extend the meaning of the word he has acquired.

# 11

# Finding out about air

One wet day Philip came into school, his cap sodden with rain. He squeezed it out into a little jug. He then began to pour the water through a funnel into a medicine bottle to find out how many tablespoons of water his cap held, but the water wouldn't go through the neck of the bottle. Philip drew the teacher's attention. 'The air's made a cork in the bottle. Why won't it let the water go in?' he asked. His teacher felt inadequate, but realised that through his interest Philip was ready to explore air. 'I'm not quite sure,' she admitted. 'But we'll do some experiments with air and perhaps we shall find the answer.'

Air is not an easy substance to learn about; we cannot see it, taste it or smell it. When it is stationary we cannot feel it or hear it either, and we can only learn about it by observing the effect it has on other substances. Yet even the youngest baby knows something about air.

The first thing the baby does on entering the world is to cry, and in so doing it takes air into its lungs. From then on it can breathe independently of its mother. The baby has now taken on a separate existence, and it will continue to breathe air in and out of its body until it dies.

From time to time the child becomes aware of the presence of air in the body. His first experience of 'wind', or air sucked into his stomach along with his food, can be very uncomfortable. At six months old he will blow bubbles from his mouth, and a baby of eleven months might pluck down from the furry trimming on a bonnet and puff it into the air.

Toddlers watching television are fascinated by the puppet koala bears with their boomerang. They enjoy helping to fly kites, are delighted by balloons, and like blowing bubbles through a straw when they drink from a bottle of milk.

By the time children are four years old they are usually familiar with aeroplanes, the flight of birds and insects, soap bubbles, and rockets which fire into space. A five-year-old will leap from a box, using an old umbrella as a parachute, and he will beg his older brother to make him a paper dart and then try to make one himself. He will plunge a bottle into the washing-up bowl and shiver with glee as the bubbles of air come to the surface.

In school we can help the child to discover more about the air which constantly surrounds him by providing equipment which will activate the air in some way. Balloons and bladders, pumps, syringes, bellows, polythene 'puffers', an old vacuum cleaner, glass jars and bottles, water and tubing, materials which float or glide, a barometer, balance pans with suitable weights such as farthings, shells and sand – all these will help him in his exploration of air.

Air is a gas, a definable substance, composed of about 78 per cent nitrogen, 21 per cent oxygen, 1 per cent argon, water vapour and $CO_2$. It can be heated and cooled, expanded and compressed; it fills any space it enters; it circulates; it supports and it exerts pressure, and it is a bad conductor of heat.

Everyday experiences offer a number of opportunities for recognising some of these properties. For instance, if a glass jar is plunged into water the water will not immediately enter the jar but waits until the air has escaped and room is made for it. Children know that air is pumped into car tyres and may have some idea of the pressure required; they may also know that pressure builds up in hot weather. Mobiles are interesting to make and to observe. Their mobility depends on the lightness of the material from which they are made, their shape and the circulating air. Perhaps father wears a string vest. Why does it keep him warm when it is full of holes? Why do we wear several layers of clothing?

Two children balanced a deflated balloon against grains of sand on the scales; then they inflated it and found they had to add more sand to balance the pans again. Air, then, has weight. The atmosphere does in fact weigh down on us at a pressure of 15 lb. per square inch. Thus we carry a very heavy weight, but we do not notice the burden because it is spread evenly about us and because it is the same as the pressure inside us. Pressure varies according to the weather and the height of the air above the sea. The pilot baling out at a great height wears a pressure suit which inflates so that he can breathe in comfort.

Although air has weight it is lighter than water, for things which contain air-filled spaces will float. Some children were experimenting with various materials to see whether they would float or sink. One child put a deflated balloon in the water. It floated beneath the water surface, but when it was inflated it rose above the water, barely touching it. The children concluded that air is lighter than water. When asked how they knew, one child replied, 'If you put a drop of water in the air it will fall.' A second child said, 'Yes, rain falls.'

Another child floated a wooden block. 'That's lighter than water,' she said. The teacher asked, 'Is it lighter than air?' 'No,' the child replied, 'If you put the block in the air it will fall.' A third observer added, 'Not many things will float in air. Only a tiny feather and smoke.'

Different kinds of wood were tested for buoyancy. Some floated more readily than others. Ebony would not float at all. 'It's too solid,' one child explained. Ebony, in fact, contains few air sacs. Water-logged wood sinks, too, as we know from wrecks lying on the sea-bed.

A pebble dropped into a bucket of water sank straight to the bottom; a boy rescued it and forced it through the neck of a balloon. He then inflated the balloon and tied the neck securely, and the inflated balloon, with the pebble inside, floated.

Onlookers then decided, 'Let's make this brick float.' (The brick was one left behind by builders.) They filled the zinc bath with water and fetched all the balloons they could find. With five balloons tied to it, the brick floated just beneath the surface of the water.

So, floating experiments multiplied. A bottle, empty and corked, floated well. Bottles with varying amounts of water were corked and compared for buoyancy. A solid glass marble sank to the bottom. 'You can make anything float if you put air in it,' the children decided. At this point the teacher took up the question of how boats, even heavy steamships, can float.

'My Dad floats at the baths,' Andrew volunteered. 'He must have air inside him.' 'How does it get inside him?' his teacher questioned. Andrew thought for a moment. He then took a noisy breath. 'Like this,' he demonstrated. 'He sucks air up.'

This was the right moment to give the children a simple explanation about the nature and function of their lungs.

The next morning Andrew brought fresh information. 'I told my Dad why he floated,' he explained. 'And he said it was respiration.' A fresh word was added to the collection of words about air.

At a later date the children were told how the fish in the aquarium tank breathed too: 'Everything that lives has to have air.' The teacher went on to suggest that this included plants and trees, but the children seemed doubtful about the plants.

Space is nearer to children than South Africa. It is there, straight above them, and they can observe it. The modern child has a concept of space which is often much more clearly developed than his ideas about Eskimos or the Sahara Desert.

Space fiction and news pictures of man's conquest of space open up many possibilities for the exploration of air, by showing what happens when there is *no* air.

The behaviour of the space pilot is determined by the atmosphere, an air canopy 200 miles deep, which envelops the earth. Beyond this protective layer, man becomes weightless and must control the temperature around him.

A baby of 14 months sees the moon in the sky and reaches for it, while clouds sailing across the sunny hilltops fascinate the four-year-old. The child in the Infant School notices the sunset, the thunder clouds and the rainbow; the firmament provides a perpetual spectacle of beauty and wonder. Weather phenomena offer limitless sources of exploration. A child of six was inspired by the loveliness of a spring day to write this poem:

> 'Blue sky, blue sky,
> White clouds, white clouds,
> All of those are very high,
> But none are higher than the sky.'

Wind bears an obvious relationship to weather. 'The wind vane points the way the wind is coming,' one child wrote about the simple wind vane she and her friends had made. Later, the child asked for an explanation of the term 'Force 8' used by the weather reporter. The teacher then described the Wind Scale, which interested the children immensely; they collected pictures which illustrated the speed of the wind (in knots): 0 = calm sea; 5 = light breeze or ripples on water; 25 = strong breeze or choppy sea; 40 = gale or clouds and heavy waves; 65 = storm or a ship in difficulties.

Keith was experimenting with water and a piece of transparent tubing. He coiled the tube into a twisted shape and then inserted both ends of the tubing under the water. The water entered the tube, but with an air bubble locked inside it. By exerting pressure on one end of the tube Keith caused the bubble to move round and round the coiled tube. He demonstrated his 'fascinator' for any spectator who paid him a visit. Keith was using air for a purpose of his own.

Man uses air, and often reinforces its use by employing power. Sailing, gliding and flying are obvious uses. Parachutes, helicopters, aeroplanes, gliders and balloons are kept suspended in the air. Rockets and jet-propelled aircraft are operated by a simple process which thrusts the craft forward through the air.

A mother brought a discarded vacuum cleaner into school. The children found it rather difficult to dismantle, and were interested in the whirring noise it made. They noticed the dusty air being drawn in, and the teacher explained that propellers whirred round and drew in the dust-laden air, and that the air was sucked through but the dust stayed behind in the filter compartment. She demonstrated the principle by sucking through a handkerchief held over the mouth.

They then went on to talk about other kinds of pumps. The teacher showed pictures and diagrams explaining how a pump lifted water by creating a vacuum. One or two children understood how the air pushed the water into the space. They then experimented with syringes, polythene 'puffers' and a hypodermic syringe, which is a pump without a valve. When at a later date the children received their polio injections, they were more interested in the instrument used by the doctor than afraid of it.

Most children are familiar with the process of inflation. They have floats and dinghies and water-wings at the seaside; some even have inflatable pools for the garden. They also inflate balloons and know that air is pumped into car tyres. The go-karts made with the help of older brothers may give them an experience of solid tyres and so help them to appreciate the increased efficiency of the pneumatic tyre.

Baking was a popular occupation in one school. Cakes were made to serve with a cup of tea on a day when mothers had been invited to visit. Great care was taken to follow the recipe, and mixtures were beaten with concentrated vigour. 'We're always having to beat things when we cook,' Judith observed.

'What other things, besides cake mixture, do we beat when we cook?' the teacher asked. They discussed the making of omelettes and soufflés, and they remembered how the cream was beaten to make it 'whipped'. The teacher reminded them of bread-making and how they had kneaded the dough.

When asked what the beating did, one child said, 'It makes the sponge cake light.'

'Watch the mixture when you beat it,' the teacher told them. 'What can you see?'

The children noticed the froth and the little bubbles. The teacher explained that beating the mixture brought air into it, and that when the cakes were cooked the air would 'swell up', or expand, keeping the particles of cake spread out, so that it was 'blown up' and light instead of solid and heavy.

When they had finished baking, the children stood the cutlery they had used in a bowl of water to soak. A child peered into the bowl.

'The knife's gone funny under the water,' she said. 'Why does it look funny?'

The teacher tried to explain. 'When the rays of light travel through the water and then through the air, they bend as they go from one to the other.' The children accepted this but queried, 'How have we got rays of light when it's a cloudy day?'

The teacher recognised the interest of the children as evidence of their readiness to understand something about light.

'There are a lot of interesting things to find out about light,' she promised. 'Light is a lovely and exciting thing to play with. I'll find you some objects which will help you to play with it.'

It is in ways like this that a sympathetic teacher can lead children on in their discoveries. In Chapter 12, the results of these and other experiments with light will be discussed, and we shall see again how many aspects of learning can spring from the same interest.

# 12

# Finding out about light

Light has always been a source of wonder and worship. An early Egyptian concept of God was Ra, the Sun God, the Giver of Life; Christians regard light as symbolic of Jesus Christ. Modern man associates the light of the sun with health-giving powers, and even devotes much time and money to sun-bathing.

The exact nature of light is still a mystery. It can be regarded as electro-magnetic vibrations which are capable of producing visual sensations. These vibrations, unlike sound, do not need a medium through which to travel. Light can travel across a vacuum: our main source of light is that which travels across an empty space to us from the sun.

A child of two will notice his shadow; by bending and stretching and dancing he can make his shadow perform. Winter sunshine produces very long shadows. A group of five- to six-year-old children measured their shadows at 2 p.m. on January 13th, and found they were between 12 and 16 feet long. At the teacher's suggestion they measured their shadows at regular intervals, but always at 2 p.m. The teacher kept a note of their findings. On February 13th the shadows had shrunk to between 8 and 10 feet, and by April they were a mere 6 feet or so; in June they were shorter still.

By this time the children were capable of making a simple

graph, representing the length of the shadows by strips of paper. They had also concluded that light travels in a straight line and 'couldn't go round a corner'.

Peter remarked, 'It gets here quickly. It gets all that way as soon as the sun shines.' His teacher told him that the speed of light was 186,000 miles per second when it was travelling through space. Peter gasped. Although his concept of speed was very immature, he did grasp something of the enormousness of this figure.

Janet offered the information, 'There's a lot about the sun in *Man Must Measure*.' She fetched the book from the library corner and turned to the pictures which showed Egyptians defining north and south by sun shadows. Discussion on defining direction by the sun followed, and the children drew the points of the compass on the school playground.

The next day they stood a pole upright on the lawn. It was a clear June day, and at the end of each hour they marked the tip of the pole's shadow with a white pebble. By the end of the afternoon the pebbles formed half an oval.

On the following day the base of the pole was encircled with a sheet of white cardboard, and the hours were marked off in lines. The children were very surprised to find that the hours were unequal distances apart.

Light is a fascinating phenomenon to explore. A reading-glass, concave and convex lenses, mirrors, binoculars, a microscope, a telescope, prisms and crystals, printing paper and sheets of glass, an old box-camera, a periscope, odds and ends of electrical equipment, and a simple lighting set are amongst the objects which can be made available on the investigation table.

The microscope is a source of joy and inspiration. Children are thrilled by the myriads of tiny gold balls seen through the microscope. Scraps of grass, hair or feathers placed under the microscope provide an entrancing experience for young children.

A glass prism will absorb a child's attention for hours,

for peering through a prism shows every object in a rainbow-tinted outline. A prism will split white light into the spectrum colours, and these can be caught on white paper or in a dark box. A second prism, placed upside-down to reverse the refraction angles, will re-form the rainbow into white light. One group of children made revolving discs in rainbow colours; when spun, these appeared 'almost white'.

Children experimenting in this way made the following observations:

'Colours come from the sunlight.'

'Sunshine is all colours, like the rainbow seen through the prism.'

'Darkness takes away the colours.'

About the school at the time were a number of art books. Manet was in favour, and children pored over the pictures, appreciating the many shades of blue used by the artist. The painting of a boy with lush, larger-than-life cherries was voted 'best'. One child remarked, 'All colours come from the sky.' The children's vital awareness of colour was reflected in their paintings.

One summer day, the headmistress appeared in school wearing a new glazed cotton skirt. It was patterned with swirls of tropical colour – flame, scarlet, gold and purple. The children gathered round and enjoyed the richness of its colours; they stroked it and handled it with great respect.

The next day the headmistress brought the skirt to school and pinned it to the wall in the hall where service was held. It provided the focal point for the service, which centred on the appreciation of light. The children responded with these comments:

'It's all light, like the Glory Light.'

'It's gorgeous. The colours are exciting.'

'It has all the colours of the sunbeam in it.'

Then one child volunteered: 'It's like the Gauguin book. It's your Gauguin skirt.'

In one class the children were looking at trees. Folders containing bark rubbings, pictures, dried leaves, scraps of bark and so on were made by the children. The teacher showed them how to make leaf prints, using daylight printing paper between two sheets of glass. The 'laurel' print was particularly beautiful.

An interest in the printing paper itself grew out of this experience. The children cut shapes of houses and people and made silhouettes. They timed the process under different conditions, discovering that it took four minutes to produce a good print on a sunny day, but that on a dull day it took thirty minutes. The prints were developed under the teacher's desk.

David was particularly interested. Following some instructions he found in a book he made a pin-hole camera from a shoe-box, a piece of printing paper, and a paper-clip.

One sunny morning he stood his camera on a table and sat on a chair in front of it. With a wrist-watch he timed himself while he sat rigid for five minutes. The result was developed under the teacher's desk, and a faint replica of David appeared on the negative. The result gave him a far greater thrill than any professional photograph would have. The teacher then brought him an old box-camera, and he and several of his friends took and developed a number of films.

The same children were introduced to a periscope. 'It's like the football match,' they decided. They toured the school, making experiments in various situations. 'You can see round the corner with a periscope,' they reported.

Experiments with a reading-glass first took the form of magnifying. One boy recorded the following in his book:
'I drew some lines on a piece of paper. When I looked through the reading-glass near to the paper I could see six lines. As I moved the glass further away I could only see three lines. So it had magnified.'

Shells, corals, flower heads and spiders were admired

under the glass. 'The magnifying glass helps you to see things better,' the children suggested. 'You really see them.'

The reflection of the view from the classroom window was thrown through the reading-glass on to the wall. The children were delighted to find the image inverted 'in glorious technicolour'.

'I know how to make another kind of upside-down picture,' a child offered. 'You do it with a tablespoon.' The teacher produced a tablespoon, so that the children could see the reflection of their faces inverted in the bowl but normal on the reverse side.

Using a concave and a convex lens and two cardboard tubes which fitted inside one another, two children made a telescope. They discovered that the best effect was obtained when the lenses were eight inches apart.

Michael was a quiet little boy who showed little interest in reading or writing. At this time the Jodrell Bank radio-telescope fired his imagination. He found an old colander and some wire in the 'make-box' and spent a long time trying to reproduce the telescope. He was anxious to 'get it right', and he sought the help of his teacher in deciphering the information he found in a book. When he had finished his model he offered to make a book about it. This was his first attempt to make a book and, indeed, to try creative writing of any kind.

Moonlight and starlight are pale reflections of sunlight at night and man has always tried to find a substitute for the powerful light of the sun. Lamps are the most ancient forms of lighting: 20,000 years ago, when Palaeolithic man decorated the Lascaux caves in France with wall paintings, he left behind him lamps of stone and grease. In primitive lamps oil for the flame was sucked up by a fibre wick from the container; modern lamps are merely an improvement on this principle. Candles are a modification of the same principle, and were used largely where oil suitable for lamps was unobtainable, as for instance in England, where candles were made by pouring melted mutton fat or tallow into a mould round a wick.

Gas from the North Sea is of topical interest. This is natural gas, and differs in origin from the coal gas more widely known. Matches, too, are a source of interest to children, and the story of their development triggered off an interest in 'What things used to look like' in one school.

Candles, used under supervision, can introduce a fresh range of experiments, such as those carried out on the following lines.

A candle was examined and a section of the wick removed. When it was dipped in water, the wick soaked it up. 'It's like a piece of string' was one observation.

Another candle was lit and the size of the flame was noticed. When the flame stood in a pool of melted wax, the candle was blown out. When it was cool it was re-lit, and the behaviour of the flame was observed.

A jam-jar was lowered over a candle standing in a saucer of water. The flame gradually went out and the water rose up the jar.

When a chimney was lowered over a lighted candle, the flame became steady and reached up the chimney. Some children measured the candle and found that it burned away half an inch in twenty minutes. They also discovered that, besides giving light, it gave off heat.

In one classroom the teacher set out a selection of electrical equipment on the investigation table – bulbs, bulb-holders, battery wire and a battery, plugs, switches and an electric bell. (Many children are far more conversant than their teachers with equipment of this kind.) A lighting set was quickly assembled. Later, when the children made a puppet theatre they equipped it with lighting, and this involved them in a measuring experience:

'The stage measures 32 inches long, or 2 feet 8 inches. We need 2 feet 8 inches of wire across the stage and 2 feet

8 inches back. 64 inches of wire. 60 inches equals 5 feet. We want 5 feet and 4 inches of wire. 5 feet 4 inches equals 1 yard 2 feet 4 inches.'

One boy asked, 'Why do we switch on the electricity to make the television picture come?' The teacher did her best to explain. 'The pictures come by light rays. In the television set there is a cathode-ray tube . . .', but her explanation petered out.

'My brother knows about television,' another boy took her up. 'He takes TV sets to pieces and makes them. He'll come and tell you all about it.' A few days later, the big brother brought a discarded television set. He removed the cathode-ray tube, and explained to the teacher and children how it worked. He left the television set but took the tube. 'It's dangerous,' he explained. 'It might explode.'

The language of light is particularly beautiful: ray, beam, gleam, moonbeam, dawn, aurora, spark, flash, blaze, flame, shine, glitter, twinkle, flare, shimmer, scintillating, translucent, transparent, limpid, glossy, iridescent.

A word collection such as this is almost poetry. Children love the sound of these words and will chant them even though they may not know their precise meaning.

A number of 'poems' were inspired by this delight in words about light. Susan, aged six, was academically slow, but she loved words. She asked her teacher to write down these 'poems' for her:

> 'The rain drops
> The silver raindrops on a spider's cobweb.'

and

> 'Candle bright, star light,
> Little Jesus, Lord of Light.'

Several stories were inspired by the discoveries children made about light. The story which follows was written by a girl of seven.

## ALL THE SUNBEAM DID

'Once upon a time there was a baby sunbeam and his mummy was the sun and he asked if he may go to the wood and play at ball but when it came to the night he was very sad for he had lost his mummy in the dark. he had lost his home.

'One day the sunbeam went to Somerset and it was raining when he got there. all the raindrops ran away when they saw him. So he turned himself into a rainbow.

'And the rainbow sat on the black cloud that took it across the sea to Africa. in Africa it was hot and it dried up all the rain and the rainbow went out of sight. And he was a sunbeam again . . .'

The story went on, filling a book of twelve pages. It was aptly illustrated.

We might call this study of light, science. We could just as readily see it as English, or art, or mathematics, or divinity. The child's discovery of the world is always an experience which involves all these disciplines.

# 13

# Finding out about sound

Graham, an intelligent six-year-old, had been ill with mumps. On his return to school he was browsing through a book on anatomy. He brought the book to his teacher, opened at an illustration of the inner ear.

'I can tell you all about this picture,' he said, and then gave his teacher a detailed and accurate account of the inner ear and its function.

'Where did you learn about the ear?' his teacher asked.

'When I was at home,' Graham explained. 'There was a senior science programme in the afternoon. It was all on there.' Further discussion revealed that Graham's father was deaf and wore a hearing aid. This had stimulated Graham's curiosity, and he was intensely interested in hearing and in the sounds he heard.

Even the very young baby is interested in sound: he loves the sound of his mother's voice, of his own utterances, of his rattle and of his spoon as he bangs it on his chair tray. One of the few things which stimulates fear in babies is sound, and a child will cry when he hears a loud or sudden noise. This initial interest in sound develops, and children begin to discriminate between sounds at a very early age. Much of what we learn depends on the way our nerves and brains interpret sound. In adults, sound can soothe, stimulate, irritate, and even cause neurosis.

Sound is the result of movement. When leaves hang still on their branches there is no sound; when they are stirred by the wind we can hear them rustle. Sound waves travel through a variety of materials at different speeds, but always much slower than light, and, unlike light, sound cannot travel through a vacuum. The sensation of sound is the effect the vibrations have on ear nerves and the brain. When the air is shaken hard, we hear a loud noise; pitch is determined by how fast the air is shaken.

Sound is comparatively easy to explore, and there is much in the everyday environment which offers starting-points. A useful collection for the investigation of sound might include some of the following: a tuning fork, alarm clocks and bells, a megaphone, discarded telephone and wireless sets, Morse signalling equipment, a gramophone, a hearing aid, musical instruments of all kinds, and oddments such as wire, gut, hollow pipes, water in glasses and bottles, wood and steel bars, shakers, and so on. In addition to the objects which make sounds, there are, of course, voices, both human and animal.

Some children, experimenting with equipment of this kind, made a number of discoveries. The teacher was invited to hold an empty tin over her ear; a tuning fork was struck and the base of the tin was touched with the vibrating fork. The effect was startling, in fact devastating, to the teacher, and when she had recovered she explained that the sound was being amplified. The operator said, 'It's like a telephone.' Following instructions which they found in a book, the children then made a tin and string telephone. When the taut string was plucked the vibrations could be seen, but not when the string was slack. The vibrating tuning fork was applied to the taut string, and the sound travelled to the receiver.

One child brought a guitar to school. He plucked the wires and watched them vibrating. 'It's like the noise a piano makes,' he remarked. He thought that the notes sounded when a hammer hit the side of the piano, so the teacher lifted off the front of the piano and showed him how, when a key is pressed, a hammer hits a string and sets it vibrating. The local education authority provided the school with an old piano, and the action was removed to the hall. Children plucked the strings, and the harps of heaven vibrated throughout the school!

Meanwhile, experiments with the tuning fork continued, and the following discoveries were made: vibrations caught on glass made the fork jig; vibrations caught on beer-bottle tops made them dance; vibrations caught on the surface of water caused it to spit, but if caught just below the surface, produced a faraway note; vibrations caught on rubber bands produced notes of differing qualities according to the tension of the band; vibrations caught on the base of a tambourine created patterns in sand sprinkled on the top of it; vibrations caught on a thumb-nail produced a note, and on the tip of the tongue they 'tickled'.

An old wireless set was dismantled, and many yards of fine copper wire were uncoiled from inside one container. A tuning fork was tried on the wire. When the wire was taut, the vibrations could be seen but not heard. Then two children stretched the wire across the room and held it near their ears. This time, when the wire was taut the vibrating tuning fork produced a sound which could be heard by both children.

Philip showed great interest in these experiments, and persuaded his father to give him an old crystal set unearthed from the rubbish in his tool-shed. Philip pestered knowledge-able people, such as the caretaker and the science master in the adjacent school, and fiddled with bits of wire for hours; finally, with his set wired to a drain-pipe, he declared firmly that he was 'receiving oscillations'.

Janice was interested in the gramophone. She had one of her own and would set the needle with great care on the revolving record. She asked what the needle did to make the sound, and was told that it followed the wavy lines in the grooves on the record. 'Gran has some records without wavy lines,' she said. In the afternoon she brought Gran to school. Gran was carrying an old-fashioned phonograph and steel discs bearing teeth. The phonograph still worked, and the sound, much like that from a musical box, was enjoyed by the whole class.

In the following week several musical boxes were brought to school, including one gem about two feet long, with eight tunes encircling its brass cylinder.

Making musical instruments is an absorbing experience at any age. Kevin hammered several nails into an upturned box, and then stretched rubber bands between the nails, producing a variety of tensions. He discovered that he had made different notes with bands of the same original length, and that those stretched 'thinner' made the 'high-up sounds', while the 'fat' bands made the low sounds. He had, in fact, discovered a basic principle – that every stretched string and every pipe or diaphragm has its own natural vibration frequency. When activated, each emits its own frequency.

Some of the simplest home-made instruments are of the percussion variety. One child brought some plastic baby-food measures. These were used in pairs: each was filled with stones, sand, rice, nails and so on, and the two were sealed together with Sellotape, thus making a maraca-shaped shaker. Together with boxes, tins and sweet cartons, painted or covered with coloured paper and likewise filled with pebbles and other items, they made a gay collection of shakers.

Clappers were made from the wooden tops of date-boxes, with empty cotton-reel holders stuck behind them. Milk-bottle tops, strung together, made bells for tambourines. One of the most beautiful-sounding gongs was a kitchen saucepan struck with a wooden spoon; the sound was improved by suspending the saucepan by a string tied to the handle.

From a stout wooden clothes-horse in the corner of one classroom were suspended a number of instruments which could be struck with a felt hammer or a wooden spoon. A range of steel tubes made chimes; flower-pots of different sizes, with thick cord knotted through the holes in their bases, made interesting bells; cups and jugs were suspended by their handles. Here it was found that shape was more important than material in determining the quality of the note. Eight orange-juice bottles, containing different amounts of water and suspended by their necks, made a water organ.

Richard experimented with water in tumblers. He adjusted the amounts until the sounds satisfied him; he then arranged and rearranged his tumblers in a row, and ran a pencil across the tops, getting different tunes. Here are some of his comments:

'That jar's got too much water.'

'If you put more water in it blocks the sound.'

'You get more sound when you've only got a drop of water.'

Several attempts to make drums produced dull, solid effects. The inner tyre from a car proved most suitable when stretched over a fairly wide tin. Some pigs' bladders, procured from a father who worked in an abattoir, were inflated with a bicycle pump. The fat was pared away and they were left to dry out for about five days. They were then moistened until they were pliable, and were next stretched over tins (solid base), a sieve (open base) and a colander. They dried taut and made excellent drums. Again, the vibrations from the tuning fork were caught on these drums with exciting effects.

In order to experiment with music-making, children need a quiet part of the school such as a spare classroom or even a corner of the school corridor. In addition to their own instruments, chime bars, a wooden xylophone, a zither and so on offer children the opportunity for making their own music.

A visiting HMI in one school was so delighted with the

tunes that the children had made that he presented them with a pentatonic harp. This is a five-note harp, C D E G A C (6 strings), any combination of which harmonise, and the player can always make a satisfying tune.

The poor acoustics in one school hall excited an interest in echoes. Children standing beyond a roof partition could not hear the teacher addressing them from the further end of the hall. In another part of the hall, by listening carefully it was possible to catch the echo of the teacher's previous word, while hearing also the one she was saying.

Out of doors, the children shouted against a wall which stood on one side of the playground, and a faint echo was heard. Some children remembered hearing echoes in a tunnel or where there were cliffs; the teacher told them that sound waves are reflected back from something which blocks them, such as a cliff or the walls of a cave. In air, sound waves travel one mile in five seconds, and it is therefore possible to calculate the distance between the source of a noise and the obstruction which reflects it.

Experiments with a tape-recorder interested children in the sounds of their own voices. They noticed, for instance, that voices are different: 'You can tell when a teacher is speaking.' 'You always know when it's a man or a lady on the telephone.' With the help of some diagrams in one of their reference books, the teacher explained to the children how their voices worked. This was followed by a discussion on animal sounds and how they are made.

A highly-prized responsibility in many schools is the job of answering the telephone. In some schools, children sign up on a rota for telephone duty when the headmistress is occupied in the classroom. An attractive book-corner occupies the telephone attendant between calls. As a rule the child will do little more than ask the caller to wait while he fetches the headmistress, but this experience gives rise to a number of questions: 'How do they get the right school? How does the sound come all that way?' 'Why do I have to put the receiver on the table when I ask the caller to wait?' 'The man said I was a clever little boy. How does he know I'm a little boy, when he can't see me?'

In some schools a field telephone system has been installed. Communication between classrooms and between the headmistress and the classrooms is established. The speech of many children who use the telephone improves tremendously; inarticulate children are often surprisingly liberated when they use the impersonal mouthpiece.

The idea of sound travelling can be conveyed to children in a number of ways. The ticking of a watch laid on a table can be heard by placing an ear against the table top at some distance from the watch. Tapping on the side of the bath can be heard when the ears are under the water. When a stone is dropped into a pond it is not the water but ripples which spread over the surface; sound vibrations travel in the same way, but they must have something to travel through, like air. Such experiments can help children to gain an elementary concept of the transmission of sound.

The language of sound can be very stirring: blare, blast, boom; din, clatter, roar; peal, bellow, clang; crack, pop, thud. Or it can be soothing: whisper, murmur; melody, symphony; harmony, musical, orchestra and opera.

The effect of sound on man's behaviour is still not clearly known. Soldiers in battle are stirred by music, and in the Old Testament David played soothing music to Saul in order to restore his sanity. There is much we can do as teachers to develop in children an appreciation of the part sound plays in our lives.

# 14

# Finding out about heat

Warmth is essential to living things. Before birth we develop in the mother's womb where the temperature is maintained at about 100° F. At birth, we must adjust to a temperature of between 68° and 70° F. In later years, we can tolerate a range of temperature between 25° and 140° F or even more, but only through adjustment of clothing. The body fights to maintain a temperature within itself of about 98° F, and we become desperately uncomfortable if this temperature varies more than a degree or two. We become miserable if we are cold, distressed if we are too hot. Heat is something which interests us at all ages, because it affects us directly and dramatically.

Teachers tend to avoid the idea of exploring heat with young children, for they often think immediately of the dangers caused by high temperature. Children can, in fact, discover much about heat without encountering temperatures higher than those which make life comfortable: heat which only excites a sensation of warmth.

Children in this country are brought up in a climate which subjects them to very wide variations in temperature. At all times of the year weather is an interesting problem. Dressing appropriately is a function which even the two-year-old understands. Jane, as a toddler, called all cosy garments 'warmint', a term she used for 'warm in it'. The five-year-old knows that he perspires when he is hot and shivers when he is cold; the six-year-old wants to know why, and he is ready to understand how perspiration helps to cool his body and how shivering is an attempt on the part of the muscles to warm him up.

The relationship between heat and other phenomena has already been mentioned. Children can observe the relationship between temperature and water and between temperature and air, as well as its association with light; baking and cooking show them what happens when food is heated. The idea that heat changes things is familiar even to the very young child.

Sometimes such changes are drastic and disastrous. The sound and sight of the fire-engine charging down the street form an event which excites curious delight in children of all ages. Charles described his reactions: 'It was all smoke like a foggy day. The fire-engine shrieked and bashed along. I wasn't harf scared. The policeman said stand back there. People rushed about. I want to be a fireman when I grow up but I'm not old enuf yet.'

Safe equipment which will help a child to understand heat is the kind which he meets in everyday life. Combustible materials used on open fires, electric and gas fires, the school heating-system, candles, tapers, lamps, a spirit stove, perhaps a Mamod steam-engine, lenses, curved mirrors and thermometers all offer opportunities for the exploration of heat.

The thermometer is a dramatic and exciting instrument. It responds readily to changes in temperature and is simple and safe for children to use. (Some of its uses were mentioned in the chapter on water.)

Vicki and Margaret were devoted to their thermometer, and for some days almost lived with it in their hands. Vicki noticed that it 'went up in two's' and suggested, 'Let's write that down.' She was thrilled to discover that this was her 'times two' table and persisted in writing it out again and

again. After recording the temperature daily for a week
he children were counting freely in two's and ten's.

Vicki and two other friends then wrote out the 'times ten'
table from the thermometer. This interest in tables grew,
and the group then worked out a number of tables. Margaret
wrote down the 'times six' table: it continued past 12 times six
to 13, 14, 15, 16 times six. The teacher, glancing over her
shoulder, remarked, 'We usually stop at twelve times,
Margaret.'

Margaret continued blissfully. 'I don't mind how far I go,'
she responded. For this group of children, tables were their
friends. At the age of six Vicki could walk into a room and say,
'It's about sixty in here. It's not very warm.'

A clinical thermometer is popular in the Wendy House;
in many homes the mother uses such a thermometer, and
children frequently mention the idea of 'having a temperature'.
One teacher explained what this meant and established the
popular idea of $98.4°$ as being normal. A seven-year-old boy
revised this information for her: with the help of his mother,
he had found out from her new 'Doctor's Book' that it could
be from $97.2°$ to $99.5°$. This information really meant something to him.

Another group of children were interested in milk and
dairy farming. The term 'scalding' appealed to them. They
repeated the word a number of times, and then asked what
it meant. Their teacher, whose home was in farming country,
brought back a dairy thermometer after the weekend. On it
the children could see 'scalding' and then 'boiling' points
marked. They compared it with the classroom thermometer
and wanted to know why it went higher.

A weather book kept in one school contained the following
entry: 'Now we have a maximum and minimum thermometer. It cost 13s. 6d. from Boots. It tells us how cold it gets
at night and how warm in the day. Minimum T night $40°$.
Maximum T day $62°$.'

Heat travels over a distance of 93,000,000 miles to earth from the sun. The sun is an enormous ball of glowing gas; although it is not the hottest planet, it is exceedingly hot – possibly about 20,000,000° at the centre. The sun was the first, and is still the main, source of the earth's light and heat. Accustomed as we are to it, we dare not look straight into it as it is too hot and too bright for the naked eye. Even the youngest child feels its meaning for man.

> 'The sun shines all day long
> It glitters as it shines
> Oh! What a beautiful thing it is!'

This was Marilyn's response to the sun one early spring day.

Clouds are a constant source of wonder to children. Observation of the weather shows them how clouds differ and what relationship they bear to the weather. They know fog and steam and they can understand something of the way in which clouds are formed.

Valerie compiled a 'Book about the clouds and the weather'. She illustrated it with photographs cut from magazines. The captions indicated her understanding of the cloud types and of their names, which she used with great delight: 'The sun and the clouds are racing shadows over the hills and the clouds are rain clouds. They are nimbus clouds . . . It is summer with cirrus clouds high in the sky.'

David, in his weather book, recorded: 'The sun evaporates the water up into the sky and makes a cloud. When the cloud gets cold rain will fall.'

An interest in holidays suggested that some parts of the earth get a greater share of sun than others. The climate in any part of the earth depends on the share of the sun's heat which it receives, on its position with regard to the sea, and on the prevailing winds.

One school possessed a huge map of the world (one of Grant's Pictorial Maps, published by Westermann). This is an outline map with pictures of people, animals, trees, crops and so on, representing life in various parts of the world. The Equator is the only line of latitude or longitude marked on it. One child, pointing to the blank space in North Africa, asked, 'Why isn't there anything there?' The teacher explained, using a torch and a globe to assist her. Deserts then became a topic of great interest to the children involved.

A large globe and a similar map in another school initiated an interest in climatic zones. Following general discussion, David wrote:

'The sun gives you light when it is daytime. When the sun goes over the other side of the world it is dark on our side. The world is constantly spinning.

'We imagine the line round the world. It is called the Equator. The hottest part of the world is the Equator.

'The sun seems to slide down the sky and set as that part of the earth spins.

'Some parts of the world is a desert or a jungle. There is no water at all (in the desert). There is a bit of water in the jungle and there are swamps.

'The coldest part of the world is the two poles. The North Pole is at the top and the South Pole is at the bottom of the world.'

This last entry offered an instructive point which the teacher used.

One day, three children asked if they could 'see the dairy thermometer work'. The teacher took them into the staffroom kitchen. Milk was heated in a pan. It rose to the top of the pan and the temperature was recorded. The reading was $110°$, and the children asked, 'Why didn't it go up to $212°$?'

On their return to the classroom, one child asked, 'Why didn't the milk boil over?' During the discussion which followed one child suggested that 'the milk must have got bigger'. The teacher introduced the word 'expanded', but the children were not at this stage able to suggest other things which expand when heated. Some months later, in hot weather, the teacher drew their attention to the telegraph wires and how they were sagging. By this time the same children were able to see that measurement with the thermometer was possible because the liquid in it expanded when heated.

Another group of children experimented with things which dissolve in water. They made this entry in their experiment book: 'Salt, sugar, soda and boracic dissolve in water. They dissolve better in hot water. You can't get them back.'

A more general interest in the way heat changes things followed. Its effect on ice and butter led to a discussion on melting, or on changing solid to liquid. One boy, whose father worked for an engineering company, had seen molten iron in a crucible. The wax in a burning candle and the making of glass products were other examples that the children considered.

While waiting for jam tarts to cook, the teacher and children discussed the use of heat to change food. 'I like raw carrot and raw turnip,' one child observed. 'But raw potato's horrid. When we heat potatoes we can make a lot of nice things like chips and mashed and jacket potatoes with butter.'

The use of wood, coal and oil for heating purposes provides examples of the way heat consumes matter. What is left after their consumption is interesting: ashes, powder, coke, charcoal are obvious products of combustion. As the children's ideas mature, by-products of coal, such as gas, aspirin, dyes and so on, are sources of interest.

In these diet-conscious days children often ask what calories are. The calorie, as used by dieticians, is the quantity of heat required to raise the temperature of 1000 grammes of water (about 2 pints) by 1° C.

Heat travels in three ways: by convection, by conduction, and by radiation. Again, it is through everyday experiences that a child comes to understand these ideas. Children in the Infant School will understand that heat travels in different ways, but full understanding of how these ways differ is not likely to develop for a few years. What children can do at this stage is to observe these experiences with greater accuracy. One teacher drew the attention of children to the way in which the mirror above the sink in their wash-corner reflected heat from the sun.

An investigation of the school heating-system led to the idea of water circulation. Reference was made to hot-water boilers used at home, and many children knew something about immersion heaters. A paper wheel was suspended by a pin over the rising column of heat given off by three candles, and it was seen to revolve. The children were next introduced to the idea of convection: when a gas or a liquid is heated in a container, it expands and rises to the top while the cool gas or liquid sinks; thus heat is carried upwards by circular movement. Although the word 'convection' was used by the teacher, it was not adopted by the children.

Why do we use a kettle-holder? Why does the poker, when it is left in the fire, get too hot to hold? Questions such as these lead to the consideration of metal as a conductor of heat; when one part of a metal object touches a source of heat, the heat spreads along the whole object. Some materials do not conduct heat very well. The use of asbestos is familiar to most children; we use wooden handles; we lag pipes; we protect water cisterns with fibreglass or other materials; we make use of bad conductors of heat, because they keep heat where we want it.

We sit in front of a fire, and on a cold day we can burn in front and freeze behind; if someone stands between us and the fire, the fire no longer warms us. Like light, radiant heat cannot turn corners; it travels through the air without heating it, and yet it warms solid objects. In a vacuum flask there is no air between the inner and outer walls; consequently there is no movement of air to promote loss of heat through convection, and the silvered walls reflect heat back into the liquid.

Man uses heat in a great many ways: to keep warm, to give light, to cook food and to do work for him. Man's body manufactures heat for him by burning up his food; this source of heat provides energy for work and for play. Ten minutes' vigorous play sends children into school perspiring, even on a cold day. When they get hungry, play begins to lose interest and they tend to feel cold easily.

The use of steam to push a piston shows how water and heat can combine to make engines work. Steam-engines in trains, ships and tractors are certain sources of interest to all boys and to many girls. A seven-year-old boy, taken to a fair for the first time, encountered a donkey-engine within five minutes of entering the fairground. Fabulous shows and breathtaking rides were completely forgotten. He spent the afternoon helping the owner to clean his engine.

Heat is one of man's greatest friends but uncontrolled it can become his most feared enemy. The understanding of fire leads to fire-prevention and fire-fighting. The intense curiosity of the child about fire is inherent in man, and this curiosity can be used as a means of helping to avoid and to remedy the effects of uncontrolled fire. For this reason, if for no other, we should encourage the child to understand heat in the form of fire from the moment he starts to be curious. Why does coal burn better when it is piled loosely? Why does slack dampen the fire? Why does a blanket or a rug put out the fire? Experiments with a candle, described in the chapter on light, include part of the answer to these questions.

The headmistress of one school wrote to the Chief Fire Officer at the local fire-station to enquire about discarded helmets, with a view to procuring one for a display. This led to personal contact, and one of the firemen agreed to visit the children in school and tell them about his work. Some lively written recording followed his visit. Words such as 'spark', 'flame' and 'blaze' were used by the children. They then made an exciting collection of 'fire words'. Such words need no two-dimensional paper pictures to illustrate their meaning. The children's imaginations supplied vivid illumination when these words were met in the reading book made by the teacher about 'The fireman and his fire-engine'.

# 15

# Finding out about the body

One of the child's earliest forms of exploration is the investigation of his own body. The only means he has of finding out where he stops and the outside world begins is through feeling his own body. Information comes to him in two ways: through external investigation, and through sensations from his internal organs and from muscles and joints. It is from the awareness of his own body that the child's idea of himself begins to develop. The bodily 'me' remains the foundation of self-awareness throughout life.

These early sources of information are confirmed and supplemented by what the child finds in the mirror and by what other people tell him. His developing use of language furthers the possibilities of investigation. Words can take him where eyes and hands cannot. By the time he is three or four the child asks many impersonal questions about his body and the way in which it functions. He accepts the behaviour of his body quite objectively.

Amongst his many questions are those connected with the appearance and function of the sex organs. The three-year-old boy isn't the least surprised to find that he differs from girls in certain parts of his body. Girls and boys are not at all concerned about the differences between them during their early years.

By the time the child enters school, sex differences are acquiring significance. The interest in outward character- istics extends to a curiosity about what happens inside. The child's natural interests are healthy. Too often the attitude of adults perverts these interests.

The arrival of the new baby or the birth of a pet's offspring awakens new interest. Sometimes a child's questions are answered honestly and simply without embarrassment, but some adults avoid the issue or provide more information than is asked for. Worse still, the child may be fobbed off with untruths.

How much a child will understand depends on what he already knows. When a child asks the inevitable 'Where will the baby come from?', or 'What are these lumps under my pussy cat?', his understanding can be assessed by turning the question back on the child. 'What do you think?' will reveal what he already understands and the exact nature of his question. The answer which satisfies will give him assurance. An unsatisfactory answer will drive the child to probe further, and unhealthy attitudes will build up if adult responses suggest there is something fishy about it all.

From time to time the Wendy House becomes a hospital. Man's world is centred on his own body and its needs. From his body and its needs man has reached out to discover his universe. The child's play reflects this intense interest in the human organism and consequent preoccupation with ill health and medicine.

On the whole, hospital play is drama in the sense that children play out adult situations, particularly those which puzzle or frighten them. The healthy child is not really interested in health or ill health as such. On the other hand, a child who suffers from chronic illnesses can discover the power they give him over others. Even at six or seven a child may actually enjoy ill health and show signs of becoming a hypochondriac.

Discovering the physical world

John fell on the rough asphalt and scraped the skin off his knee. A week later the scab had dropped off, and only pale, scarred skin remained. 'I've grown some new skin,' John said thoughtfully. 'How did it come?' His teacher helped him to find an answer to his question in an illustrated *Book of the Human Body*. John's interest was throughly aroused and he pored over other diagrams in the book, asking endless questions. He tried to reproduce a diagram illustrating the network of blood vessels circulating the body. 'It's just like a tree,' he explained.

A headmistress chose as her theme for service the unique nature of the individual. The fact that she had known more than two thousand children and never seen two who looked exactly alike gave rise to interested comments: 'I'm like our big girl,' Gloria volunteered. 'And me Mum says we take after our Dad.' This opened the way to discussion about the characteristics we inherit and the way in which we differ, in spite of the fact that we all have the same physical complement. Children who were less favoured in some respects than others were shown how individuality means that we all have different qualities. Some of the prayers written by children for use in service during the rest of the week reflected their appreciation of individual differences. 'In this world there are all kinds of things and all kinds of people. Celia has red lips and golden hair and she is beautiful. I have only brown hair and little eyes but I can sing and make good tunes . . .'

One class made charts to show the colour of eyes and hair. They discovered that fair hair predominated and that there was only one red-head amongst them. Eyes tended to be blue more often than any other colour. Linking this investigation with their exploration of touch (described later in this chapter), they made hand-prints and finger-prints, using a Padawax pad, and saw how very different these prints were. They then realised the significance of finger-prints in crime detection.

The presence of a few immigrant children in the school led to a consideration of why people in other countries were sometimes unlike English people in the colour of their skin and the shape of their features.

A scrap-book containing pictures of things that are 'Good to Eat' started an interest in food and its passage through the body. Most children of school age have some understanding of their food tube and of the way in which they swallow food and excrete waste. They know that they differ from plants in this, but they have little concept of digestion. 'Why do we eat, if it's going to come out at the other end?'

Most children at this stage know that they eat in order to grow. The five-year-old may think that the food travels more or less directly to his arms and legs. The six-year-old will grasp something of the digestive process, particularly if he is shown a simple diagram of the alimentary canal. The seven-year-old will know that when he is very hungry he gets tired and that food will revive him. Few children at the Infant School stage really grasp the idea of energy and replacement of tissue in connection with food.

At about the age of six children lose their milk teeth. Occasionally a loose tooth frightens a child. He may need reassuring that his permanent teeth will appear. On the whole, the shedding of milk teeth is welcomed as a stage on the way to maturity. Many children will wiggle their teeth in order to loosen them. Some treat a tooth which falls out with great respect and will often insist on wrapping it in a handkerchief and taking it home. Some parents reinforce this attitude by recognising the loss of each tooth with a sixpenny piece.

Such an event furthers the child's understanding of digestion and the important part played by the teeth, particularly if chewing becomes a problem for a few days. He will become interested in the way his teeth grow, and this is the time to show him how to care for them. The significance of various foods is also of interest. One book about 'The Food We Eat', compiled by two six-year-old children, contained pictures grouped under the following headings: 'Foods which help us to grow', 'Foods which keep us warm', 'Foods which give us energy to play'.

In the chapter on air we saw how children become aware of their lungs and pressure inside the body. Most children of five or six think of breathing as something which takes place in the nose or mouth and head. As they grow older they notice what happens when they run, when they blow up a balloon, or when they have a heavy cold. They know about the breathing apparatus worn by deep-sea divers and astronauts. It isn't until the child is about seven, however, that he realises that in order to stay alive he must breathe.

A stethoscope was provided with a nurse's outfit for the Wendy House. Children were soon using it 'to listen to the heart'. They discovered that the heart never stopped. With the aid of a stop-watch, they found out how many beats there are to the minute (about 70). They discovered that it went much faster after running or skipping. 'It's very busy,' they said, and grasped the idea that it was busy 'sending the blood round'.

Peter climbed on top of the wall round the boys' toilets and fell off. The children brought him into school. He was moaning and cradling his forearm, which was arched like an upturned bow. A few days later he appeared in school with his broken arm in a plaster. He became a hero and collected various decorations on his plaster. He explained to his admirers that he didn't need a new arm. He'd only broken the bone and that would mend itself.

Onlookers started feeling their own limbs. Their teacher borrowed a jointed lay-figure from the secondary art room and showed the children how their bones were jointed. With the aid of rubber strips from a bicycle tyre she tried to explain how muscles activated the limbs by pulling on the bones.

A simple investigation derives from the use of the senses. We have already paid some attention to the investigation of sight and hearing in the chapters on light and sound. The School Medical Examination will often initiate an interest in sight. Following this experience in one school, a 'tester' was made for the domestic corner. After spending some time in testing and recording, one child asked, 'Why do we have two eyes?' His teacher borrowed an old bioscope from her grandfather and used it to illustrate the way in which two eyes help us to see things as solid. With their interest thus aroused the children went on to compare the human eye with the camera they had used in the light experiments.

Derek was fitted with a hearing aid. The unfamiliar sounds he now experienced sometimes worried him. When children became noisy he would complain, 'If they don't stop making that noise, I shall switch off.' His friends were curious and wanted to know why he couldn't hear properly. The answers made a link with the work done about sound and vibrations. The children were intrigued by a diagram of the ear and the function of the ear-drum.

Experiments to test hearing were carried out. A watch was held level with one ear and the children recorded the distance from which its ticking could be heard. They found that these distances varied and that for some people one ear was more responsive than the other. Blindfolded, the children tried to locate the sound of two pencils clicking together. They were amazed to find that they were unable to discriminate between sounds directly in front of them and those directly behind.

A selection of 'things to smell' was set out on a tray. The game of identifying them, with and without a blindfold, was popular for a time. The children discovered that they could 'nearly taste some smells', and that smell and taste often disappeared when they had a heavy cold. They made books about 'Things I like to smell'.

The sense of touch was explored by the exciting experience

of handling different textures when blindfolded. Experiences of this kind added words to the children's vocabularies and helped them to clarify the meaning of some of the words they already knew. For example, one child, feeling a glass paperweight, described it as 'soft'. She didn't know the word 'smooth'. Once she had discovered it, she spent some time finding other things which were smooth. The child lives in a world of tasting and smelling, of seeing and hearing, and it is these experiences that make up 'sense'.

During his early years in school the child goes through a stage of intense physical activity. His limbs have learned to co-ordinate, and he is becoming increasingly skilful in co-ordinating his finer muscles. Girls will practise complicated dancing steps and skipping for hours. Increasing muscular control delights the child and he will perform quite difficult feats on the climbing apparatus. He uses tools with great dexterity, and it is a great pleasure to watch him use his hands.

Children abound in energy. Skilful movement and abundant energy need adequate modes of expression, and the child will love the person who really satisfies his physical needs. He will take every opportunity to demonstrate his skill, and by the time he is seven he will enjoy competing with other children and trying to break his own records.

This increasing awareness of the body and its potential can be used by the teacher in the movement lesson. The child of six or seven knows something about his own shape and the shapes his limbs can make. He knows how the various parts of his body move, and he has some understanding of the space in which he moves. He knows the names of many parts of his body – 'elbow' and 'knee', 'shoulder' and 'hips', et cetera – and these are words the teacher can use to channel his attention. He knows words which denote quality – 'heavy' and 'light', 'fast' and 'slow'. His vocabulary includes words such as 'curved', 'spiral', 'stretched', 'sharp' and 'spiky'. He knows how to keep still. Physical consciousness gives more meaning to his movements, and the work done by children of this age is completely uninhibited, an expression of their joy in being alive.

What a child knows about his body is often conveyed by the pictures he draws. Young children draw what they know rather than what they are expected to see. In their pictures they emphasise what is important to them. In a self-portrait a child may draw his inner organs or his prominent teeth, or what he knows about the way his voice works.

During his first years in school the child becomes fully aware of being alive and of the difference between animate and inanimate objects. The toddler thinks that objects feel as he does, and will blame the table for having hurt him. At a later stage, anything which seems to move – the sun, the wind, an aeroplane – is thought to be alive. But the six-year-old is aware of the differences between animals and people, which move of their own will, and balls or buses, which must be activated from without.

This awareness of life is related to a growing understanding of death. Jane's little dog Sandy was run over. Jane described him lying dead in the gutter as 'Just like Sandy used to be but with all the Sandy gone out of him'.

In some districts the drabness of day-to-day living is relieved by a few great moments. The wedding and the funeral are the dramatic highlights of life, and everyone, from toddler to grandpa, is involved. The ceremony of 'laying-in' is still retained in many down-town neighbourhoods. Small children as well as adults visit the home of the deceased and pay their respects to the flower-decked coffin.

'Cowboys and Indians' is a popular game among six- or seven-year-olds. Killing is an essential part of the drama and the person who is killed must remain absolutely motionless. The 'dead' child plays his part with complete concentration. He is trying to find out, by the only means possible to him, what it feels like to be dead.

A five-year-old looked at her grandmother and said: 'You're nearly dead now, aren't you, Grandma?' She associated death with old age. The seven-year-old, who has witnessed killing quite frequently on television, will know that death can happen at any age. He is not particularly worried about death and tends to regard it as an inconvenience or a deprivation when he loses a relative or a friend. He misses the friend who shared his games or the grandmother who used to give him chocolate, but he doesn't actually mourn.

This natural interest of the child in his body and its functions, in life and in death, will remain of primary importance to him throughout his life. The teacher of young children is responsible for helping the child to acquire a sound knowledge of his physical self, and so to establish healthy attitudes in adult life.

# 16

# Finding out about the way things work

Much of man's life is devoted to conquering his environment. Human sources of energy are limited, but man's ingenuity has enabled him to find ways of extending the use of his hands. The machines he invents allow him to exert great force with little movement. Often the machine does the work for him, provided that his brain controls it. One of man's nightmares, used in science fiction, is the idea of machinery taking on an independent existence and exerting power over man.

Few interests can rival the observation of machinery in action. No story can compete with the arrival of a helicopter. Even water play is abandoned when the concrete mixer gets busy outside or when the crane on the nearby construction site is operating. A derelict motor-car on a rubbish tip is a symbol of mystery and magic to any small boy. Boys and many girls of all ages are entranced by the activities of clockwork toys.

Machines do not create energy in themselves. A machine works because energy is poured into it. Long before a child understands mechanical principles he devises ways of using energy more effectively.

No baby is able to lift a cider barrel and put it on top of a box, but he *can* push a little barrel up a plank and so settle it on the top. He discovers that bricks are bulky and heavy to carry, so he fetches a barrow and piles them into that. He is unable to lift a bucket filled with sand, but if he ties a skipping-rope to the handle and passes the rope over a rung of the climbing frame the bucket is easily lifted. In each case the child is using a machine which concentrates energy and enables him to use such force as he possesses with maximum efficiency.

One of a teacher's most precious aids is a collection of 'things which work'. Most of the items in this collection cost nothing: an old lock and key, taps and washers, zip-fasteners, ball-bearings, screws, coils, springs and wheels, cogs and a driving chain, pulleys, wedges, bar and horse-shoe magnets, a jack, hinges, bells (alarm-clock, door bell, bicycle bell), and levers. Screwdrivers of different sizes are, of course, essential. Such items provide an exciting source of exploration for children of all ages.

The introduction of synthetic materials has opened up fresh possibilities for the use of familiar principles. A visit to the toy counter of a chain-store will produce a wide variety of toys which operate because of the nature of the material from which they are made. We find, for instance, fashioned in plastic, hens which lay eggs, sewing-machines which pop up, vehicles equipped with many devices including the ejection of the driver, and plenty of other simple machines. The investigation of such a collection could challenge the mechanical understanding of the most intelligent child.

The wheel can encourage a study of wide-ranging interests. Palaeolithic man lived by hunting and had no need for the wheel. When man started to live in cities, food had to be transported and he set about devising ways of doing this. The rich land of Egypt and Mesopotamia produced food easily, and man here was free to serve the community in many ways. In Egypt food could be transported by water, but in Mesopotamia cities were scattered all over the plain, and here we find wheeled vehicles being used before 3000 B.C.

The history of the wheel and of the way in which machines of all kinds have come to depend on it is only one aspect of this fascinating topic.

An interest in wheels was initiated by one teacher working with seven-year-old children. She arranged a display of wheels taken from many situations in everyday life. In her display she included a spinning-wheel, a potter's wheel, a gramophone, wheels from a clock, from sewing-machines and from clockwork toys, cogs and the gear-box of a car, a mill-wheel and a cart-wheel, a bicycle, pictures of windmills, grinding wheels, turbine wheels and a paddle steamer; there was even a Catherine-wheel from a box of fire-works. She collected good reference books to enable the children to follow up their first-hand observations. She hired a film on the history of the wheel.

For two or three days children handled the different wheels and discussed them and their functions in a somewhat random fashion. One boy brought in a car tyre he had found on a piece of waste ground and became interested in the pneumatic tyre. By the end of the week the children were forming groups each centred round some particular interest suggested by the materials.

One prominent interest was the motor-car. An old car provided by a parent stood on the playground, with some parts such as the windows removed for safety, and became a rich source of investigation and imaginative play for the rest of its life. A great moment came when a teacher's car refused to start as she was leaving for home in the evening.

Seven-year-old mechanics gathered round, offering advice of all kinds. Their main aim was to get the bonnet up. 'Perhaps the distributor's wet, Miss . . . It's the starter-motor what's gone . . . The plugs aren't firing . . .'

Geoffrey, a thoughtful observer, offered his help when all else failed. 'Perhaps it's the petrol, Miss. It won't go without petrol.' He had solved the problem.

With the aid of corrugated cardboard strips pasted round empty cheese boxes, one group of children experimented with cogs. Amongst the equipment in their classroom was a plastic clock face with a cog mechanism behind. Using this as a model, they devised a working toy duck which waddled.

A bicycle gave rise to an interest in ball-bearings. The father of one child worked in the local cycle factory, and he sent into school a variety of bearings, both spherical and cylindrical. The children acquired some understanding of friction and of how it was reduced in machinery.

During the weekend one child went on a day-trip to the seaside. The journey took him through Alford in Lincolnshire, where a working windmill still grinds corn. He brought back a diminutive sack of flour, a recipe for stone-ground wholemeal scones, and a vivid description of his tour of the works.

Following this report a subsidiary interest in measuring journeys to various seaside resorts sent the children in search of a wheel 'exactly three inches round', for use in translating the distance as shown on the map according to the scale. Then the teacher supplied an assortment of wheels and suggested that the children might like to measure them, round and across, and record the results. Eventually the children drew up the following table:

OUR WHEELS

| Round. | | Across. | |
|---|---|---|---|
| | Nearly 8 inches | | Over $2\frac{1}{2}$ inches |
| | Nearly 12 inches | | Over $3\frac{1}{2}$ inches |
| | Nearly 29 inches | | Over $9\frac{1}{4}$ inches |

From this table they abstracted the mathematical idea that 'Round is about three times across'. They tested their deductions, using a tape measure, on every round and cylindrical object they could find. The teacher was able to introduce the use of callipers to solve the problem of measuring across a round object.

A more obvious interest centred round road vehicles and

what they carried. The school was situated near a busy road, and a student on teaching practice took a group of six-year-old children to record the type of vehicle using the road, what it carried and, where possible, its destination. Small pictures of vehicles, prepared by the teacher, helped the children to make their records. On return to the classroom, the pictures were used to make a series of simple block-graphs:

Number of lorries, vans, etc., passing between 9 and 10 a.m.

Vehicles carrying food, clothing, furniture, etc.

Number of private cars passing in either direction between given times.

Julie tried to make a pram for her doll. She used a tomato crate and four wooden wheels which she tried to nail directly onto the bottom of the crate. The nails split the wood and the teacher suggested that screws wouldn't split the wood in this way. Julie then fastened on her wheels with screws, which served for a few hours. Observers offered other solutions: 'It should have a bar thing across.' Eventually Julie screwed her wheels to a wooden axle. 'It looks better,' she agreed. The pram lasted for nearly two weeks.

One of the most familiar pieces of mechanism is the clock. Discarded clocks, provided by a clock-mender, were a constant source of interest. The youngest child enjoys watching the works go round and tries to find out what makes a clock tick. He does this as a rule by taking the clock to pieces, and this is perhaps as far as he will go until he is about seven years old and his thought processes have become more definitely structured. At this stage the child will enjoy trying to reassemble the clock or even making things which run on clockwork.

David, aged seven, loved clocks and watches. He acquired a number of them as presents or swops from many sources. With the aid of a small screwdriver he took them to pieces, and with infinite patience sorted out the various parts, right down to the smallest screw. At home his dressing-table was devoted to innumerable bits of mechanism. His prize exhibits were a wheel operated by sand running from a hopper, and a crane with an extendible jib, mounted on a turntable.

A profitable source of interest and discovery is the work of people who use machines. Every environment offers a different range. On the new housing estate we see the bulldozer at work, along with excavators, concrete mixers, plumb-line and spirit-level, drills and carpenters' tools. Children who work in down-town schools may live near a railway station, where signals, turntables and engines are busy. The country child has access to machinery used for milking, ploughing, and harvesting. A dockland environment has derricks and cranes, steamships and a variety of machines which transport goods.

Everywhere we see roadworks, with pneumatic drills, bulldozers, steam-rollers and tar-spreaders. In every kitchen the child can observe machines of many kinds, including washing-machines, spin-driers, egg-whisks and food-mixers. One plastic potato-peeler is operated by a cycle of cups into which water is driven through a hose attached to the sink tap. This gadget illustrates the principle which operates a water-wheel. Some of these gadgets can be introduced into the classroom.

Sometimes workers in the community can be persuaded to visit the school and talk to the children about their work. We have already considered enlisting the help of firemen (Chapter 14) and one school took such an experience a stage further. A fireman friend arranged for the fire-engine itself to visit the school. It stood on the school playground while the children clustered round and listened in awed silence to the fireman, who described how the various parts work. The children's questions came later in the day, and each child gained from the experience at his own level. The operation of the ladders engaged the keen attention of the more able seven-year-olds. Many of the younger children merely played out the drama of fire-fighting again and again.

Children in another school are allowed to visit the fire-station opposite and to watch the firemen cleaning and repairing their equipment.

Many schools have meals cooked on the premises, and the kitchen abounds in interesting pieces of machinery. Small groups of children can visit it to watch mixers, potato-peelers or dish-washers at work.

The piano-tuner, the joiner with his brace and bit, the caretaker replacing a used washer on a tap or mending a fuse, are all sources of learning for young children. Attitudes of respect for these workers in the community are encouraged by an understanding of what they do. This is in itself an essential part of a child's education.

Many children possess bicycles or similar chain-driven vehicles. Learning about the way they work will help the child to take care of his vehicle. The care and maintenance of any such vehicle should be the responsibility of the owner at any age.

Most districts have a factory or industry. Children from one school, situated in the centre of a city, visited a furniture factory, the packing department of a stocking factory, a cardboard box factory, and the signal-box in a railway station. Children living in a rural area visited a saw-mill, a brickyard and a pea-canning factory. In each case the local library assisted by lending appropriate reference books to the school.

Such experiences are not necessarily recorded in the form of words and pictures in books. The creative use of waste materials takes on a fresh dimension, and the accuracy of the child's observation is revealed in the detail of his constructive work. Aeroplanes must have proper propellers, a castle has a drawbridge which can be operated by a piece of string, and the railway track has a series of signals which function. Many children find that more is achieved when they work in pairs or small groups. One or two inventive children begin to take the lead.

Many women teachers who are not mechanically minded may hesitate to embark on discovery of this kind. Those who venture into it often find that their inadequacy proves to be no barrier to the child's learning. So great is the curiosity of most children in things which work that good material and a permissive environment may be practically all the teacher need provide.

# 17

# Beginning to understand geography

Many children, from their earliest days, have a burning desire to see what is round the next corner. As soon as a child is able to crawl across the carpet to the door he feels an urge to prise it open, because the unfamiliar hall beyond would seem to be more interesting than the room he knows. By the time he is two years old even the garden no longer satisfies his curiosity, and his mother ties him to the drain pipe by knotting a clothes line round his waist; otherwise his sense of adventure would carry him fearlessly beyond hope of finding his way home.

Penny, aged two, loves accompanying her parents to see Grandma, who lives 150 miles away in Wales. Experience of the hours of travelling has given her some idea of what a 'long way' means. When friends of the family emigrated to Australia, she was told that she wouldn't see them again until she was a big girl, because she would have to fly in an aeroplane over the sea and over a lot of countries in order to visit them. Penny expressed her idea of this fact as, 'Kim lives in Australia now. That's a long way away like Grandma in Wales.'

When Timothy was barely twenty months old he could recognise the road he lived in and adjacent streets. He would bounce excitedly in his pram when he approached a familiar road on the way home from the shops. By the age of four he knew the main streets in his home town and the direction of the bus routes into town from his home in the suburbs. He also remembered picnic spots in the country and loved to anticipate landmarks on the way to them. One day, when visiting a friend's house with his mother, they took an unusual route. He looked puzzled and asked, 'Are we lost? Never mind. We can look for that tall building and then we shall know where we are.' A number of places were associated with his personal experience. Birmingham was known as 'where Uncle lives', and a certain road as 'the street where I counted three red doors.' Association is an important factor in recognition, particularly the association of people with places.

It is in this innate interest in exploring and identifying one's environment that geographical ideas are rooted. Geography can be defined as a description of the earth, and geographers are earth-lovers. Young children notice and are interested in what they find on the earth. In the early stages it is in the 'what?' rather than in the 'why?' that this interest centres, and as adults we can help children to observe carefully and to describe accurately what they find. A firm concept of geography is slow to develop and needs to be founded on accurate observation. When children ask for explanations, we should give them as simply as possible, without talking down. They will comprehend according to their level of maturity, assimilating as little or as much of our explanations as is within their understanding. To tell a child when he asks 'What makes rain?' that 'The clouds are crying', or that 'Somebody has squeezed the spongy clouds', is inaccurate and an insult to his intelligence. We can explain the rain-cycle as simply as possible, showing the child how water evaporates from the wet playground when the sun shines, or how condensation forms on the cool window-pane in a hot room. He will understand perhaps only a little of what we tell him. Later he will ask the question again, when further experience and greater maturity of thought will enable him to extend his understanding.

The child brought up in a rural area has, perhaps, a simpler task than the child who lives in a large town. There are excellent starting-points for either child, but the complexities of urban geography are more difficult to grasp.

Man is becoming increasingly mobile, and many children today travel about with their parents, particularly at holiday times. They share with their parents the experience of consulting a map and of driving along fast roads which open up the countryside. Some children travel by air and see the familiar land reduced to a plan beneath them. Many travel overseas, and words describing travel and direction become part of their active vocabulary. Indeed young children often learn to interpret road signs before they learn to read. They may know crossroads and T-junctions before they can recognise the symbols which stand for numbers.

Even the child who spends most of his life near home is interested in the journey he takes to school. He may try to reproduce it, using a combination of pictures and plans. He realises, as Peter did, that 'If I'm going to get all that lot on this little piece of paper, it'll have to be small.' Scaling down reality is the solution and often comes naturally to the child, because he is already familiar with the idea of scale through playing with toys. More and more parents are buying their own homes, and the family may spend hours exploring the plan of a new housing estate before visiting it and seeing it come to life.

Many children learn to understand a simple plan or map by trying at first to make their own. 'The roads that lead to school', 'Where we live', 'A plan of our school' will enable them to see how the geographer begins to solve the problems of representing large three-dimensional features in two dimensions on a small piece of paper. A globe is found in many classrooms and it fascinates children, at first because it spins. Later they come to regard it as a symbol of adventure, and their understanding of what it stands for is enlarged when they watch television programmes which show them what the earth looks like to the man in space. The roundness of the earth, which from experience appears to be so flat, is a difficult concept and may be late to develop. Direction is also a problem to many young children, and in spite of the fact that most small boys at some time carry a compass in their pockets, the points of the compass remain a mystery. Why, indeed, should North become associated with the top of a map? And where does the north wind come from?

Modern machinery enables man to cut through a hill with comparative ease and speed. The profile of the crust of the earth as seen from a motorway shows layers of rocks of different kinds, topped by a thin layer of soil. Helping to dig the garden confirms to the child the extreme thinness of that layer of soil on which life depends. Exploring a quarry extends the story, and a child may begin to understand how the various layers can curve or fracture.

A stream is a source of great joy to a child. He can dam back the water and watch a reservoir begin to form. He can follow the winding course of the stream and notice how it eats away the bank on the outer side of the curve. Wading shows him where the stream runs deeper and swifter, and his paper boat may be caught up in the current. Ideas about erosion and the way in which streams and rivers sculpture the face of the earth are extended when the child visits the seashore and finds the pebbles and sand brought down from the land.

Mountains are another source of wonder to small children. A panting climb to the summit offers some experience of height. The contrast between the cold barren peaks, bereft of soil and vegetation, and the lush rolling meadows in the valley tells an important story which the child, with the help of an adult, can understand.

What grows and lives on the crust of the earth intimately concerns the child, and shops or market-places are as profitable a starting-point as a farm. The open market of a town, large or small, offers a wealth of material. The child of six knows that oranges and pineapples don't grow in Daddy's back-garden, and that Californian plums, New Zealand butter and Florida grapefruit owe their names to those places over the seas from which they come. In a local market the produce of neighbouring farms is offered for sale. Its character changes according to the season, and the man who sells home-grown tomatoes and fresh green peas in August is found selling sacks of potatoes and cooking apples a few months later.

These people bring what they grow, and sell it. Sometimes there is an exchange of commodities and the idea of trade, which depends on the production of surplus goods, begins to dawn in the child's mind.

Sometimes the market or shop offers strange and exotic fruits and vegetables, such as yams, avocado pears and green peppers, which suggest an unfamiliar way of life and speak of remote foreign lands. The child's knowledge of vegetation starts with what he sees in neighbouring gardens. His knowledge of animals starts with pets. But he needs to extend this knowledge to include the rich produce of tropical plantations or the fascinating animal life of Australia. A sound knowledge of the familiar will render him capable of reaching out intellectually to the farther parts of the earth.

As teachers and parents, we too often fall into the trap of forcing facts on a child the moment his interest awakens. When helping a child to grasp difficult concepts time is essential, and if we try to rush him he will finish up with distorted and stunted ideas.

Much of the child's understanding of geography depends on his sense of wonder about natural features and phenomena. The sheer poetry of the earth with its majestic mountains and turbulent rivers, its ever-changing contours, its rich abundance, its arid rocks and its lush farmlands, should remain a permanent source of beauty and variety. As adults we can help the child to become sensitive to and appreciative of these things, so that he learns to comprehend as fully as possible the miracle of the earth and of the life springing from it.

In many of our large towns we find schools in which something like 50 to 70 per cent of the children come from other countries. In one class of six-year-olds there are children from Spain and Italy, China and Japan, India and Pakistan, Jamaica and Mexico. We have collected here representatives of many parts of the earth, each bringing experiences and customs he can share with others. The teacher of this class encourages the children to sing the songs they have learned from their parents, to repeat poems and stories from their own countries, to dance according to their native tradition, and to play the games they know. When they are able to, they describe in English what they remember of their native land. Around the classroom are displayed many examples of clothing, utensils and tools brought by the children. Their languages are another source of interest to the whole school. One little West Indian boy made a Jamaican kite, using flexible willow twigs and coloured tissue paper. He discovered a fresh respect for himself when other children referred to him as an authority on kites. In spite of a meagre English vocabulary, he had found a means of communication, and his friends caught a glimpse of an unfamiliar land through him.

Nearer home, people living in the same street work at different jobs. An exchange of information about fathers' jobs in one school led to invitations to some of these fathers to visit the school to talk to the children about their work. This interest in people at work extended to many aspects of the community and then to the work of people in other lands.

The child whose father worked as a carpenter in a local furniture factory was fascinated by the story of the lumberjack.

The romance of people and their work comes to children in story form by film and television. The live adventure of Sir Francis Chichester in the *Gypsy Moth* sparked the interest of seven-year-old boys in tales of exploration, and Marco Polo, Columbus, Livingstone and Scott became heroes. These children were filled with a sense of awe and respect for the people whose courage has helped us to extend our knowledge of the earth.

When considering the way in which children find out about water and air, and light and heat (Chapters 10, 11, 12, 14), the persistent importance of weather phenomena was brought to their attention time and time again. The young child feels rain fall on his head. He sees and enjoys the rainbow. He watches great clouds form and re-form as they roll across the side of a mountain. He laughs when the wind bundles him along the road. He squeals with delight when the snow is deep enough to go over his Wellington boots. He is fascinated by the devastation left in the wake of flood waters. He mourns when his seedlings wilt in the drought. What he observes absorbs his interest, and only as he begins to understand does he begin to ask 'why?' He needs many and varied experiences of weather before he is ready to accept and comprehend even a simple explanation of a complicated phenomenon such as rain.

Children who have lived through six or seven years of English weather have acquired a vast array of information about climate. They have personal experience of sun 'hot enough to split the stones', of 'icicles 14 inches long', of thunderstorms and gales, of floods and 'official' droughts. The very wide range of climate experienced in this country enables the child to understand the climatic conditions which exist in many other parts of the earth. He knows the effects of prolonged sunshine and of prolonged rain, and the way in which life changes according to the time of the year. He is equipped to accept the story of people who need little clothing, of people who depend on sledges for transport, of the children who dance naked in the rain when it falls. There is something familiar about the different ways of other people. The fascination of learning that people do similar things and use similar tools but with those differences which make life seem strange to the English child, opens the way to learning about people in all parts of the world.

As understanding develops, the child's own vocabulary can set his mind enquiring. His Fair Isle cap and Shetland pullover, his moccasins, the Shantung silk dress his mother wears, Volkswagen cars, Swedish glass, and goods stamped 'Made in Tokyo' acquire new meaning.

As his knowledge extends, the immense scale of things will continue to amaze him. He will comprehend the spectacle of the Victoria Falls, the terrible challenge of Mount Everest, the fathomless mystery of the ocean deeps, the fearful expanse of the Sahara desert and the impenetrable depths of unexplored jungle and swamp. Space travel, even science fiction, will show him an ever-increasing universe, extending beyond the powers of imagination. He will grow increasingly aware of the wonder and, at the same time, of the reality of the earth he inherits.

As parents and teachers we can help the child to retain and develop this sensitivity, and we can encourage him to make every effort to observe and record with accuracy. We can offer him means of expressing his experiences and, by helping him to become articulate about his earth, so to grow fully appreciative of it and of what he owes to it. In time he too may become, in every sense of the word, a geographer and a lover of the earth.

# 18

# Beginning to understand history

Ideas about history are slow to develop, for a sense of time, which is one of the most difficult of concepts, is crucial to its understanding. An understanding of time involves ideas about succession, duration and rhythm. Of these, rhythm is perhaps nearest to the nature of the child.

The pattern of history reflects the pattern of time which underlies the order of the universe, and the points made in Chapter 7 about the child's developing sense of rhythm are closely related to his developing sense of history. The child becomes more aware of the systematic ordering of events as he experiences the rhythm of the seasons, of birth and death, of his own body, and of the ebb and flow of the tide. It is in living the rhythm of life that the child's sense of balance and sequence dawns and develops.

The succession of events may be more readily understood than their duration. A child of six can tell you the exact sequence of events in his day, but he may have little idea of the duration of each, and he may feel that it took him much longer to wash his hands than it did to watch a ten-minute film on television. The child brought up in a methodical home, where the family timetable is firmly established, is likely to develop a respect for order and will expect to find ordered sequence in the events of history. The child who lives on a farm, for instance, where the pattern of the days revolves round feeding and milking, ploughing and sowing and reaping, irrespective of holidays or Sundays, is more likely to appreciate the inevitable order in man's affairs than the child brought up in a home where life is more casual.

There are a number of ways in which links with the past are forged for the child. It is perhaps through his relationships with people that he first senses the existence of these links. Within the life of the family the child associates with adults from different generations. Mother, grandmother, even great-grandmother, present him with a personal picture of life as it was lived in different ages. The people in his family offer him a personal channel of communication; he finds preserved in their behaviour old-fashioned attitudes and beliefs, and although he may discredit or even ridicule the ideas which Gran has about the way in which he should live and behave, he is made aware that ideas change.

It is through his contacts with older people that the child acquires his cultural beliefs and customs. They transmit to him a way of life which makes him a part of the pattern of history, and he learns his way of life as much from the influence of adults as he does from friends of his own age. If among those adults there is one whose own enthusiasm for history is well developed, the child's own sense of history will be fired, and his life will become enriched by the knowledge of what he inherits.

Village life often provides the child with a close-knit group in which there are adults outside his own family who are concerned about him and who influence him. It is easier to see historical patterns in a small, slow-paced community where there are successive layers from different generations existing contemporaneously. A child here lives his history as he grows and plays; he encounters the past in his immediate life.

Parents who hoard offer the child a rich source of historical interest. Tools and utensils, furniture and clothing, trinkets and treasures of all kinds are eloquent reminders of the people who used them. Keeping things from the past establishes a sense of tradition in a home, and the child understands the message conveyed by objects which are familiar and yet different. The wooden rocking-chair, assembled without nails or screws and polished with loving care, obviously deserves his respect. As he runs his fingers over the worn rocker, he glimpses the generations of old ladies who have used it, and in doing so he is linked physically with bygone days.

Possessions which have been preserved with veneration provide a rich opportunity to learn history. Many adults may remember stone hot-water bottles, or that marble slab from the days when there were no refrigerators, those wooden butter-pats, that copper preserving-pan, the wooden flour-scoop, perhaps even a wooden foot-warmer with its receptacle for a hot-water bottle and its beaded tapestry lid. Tools from yesteryear provoke questions and, if a little imagination is used, provide the answers. Old china and crockery preserve pictures of life as it was in other days. The people who used these possessions seem close and are easily imagined.

A rich source of family history is, of course, the photograph album. In some homes, too, the child finds old editions of books, old prints, perhaps concert programmes and old magazines, even 'in memoriam' cards, which spell out the life of other times. Christmas cards are a source of great pleasure to children, and we frequently find traditional detail preserved in their designs.

At the age of seven Alison is fascinated by a leather-bound volume of *Girls' Own* magazines, dating back to 1889. She finds the advertisements particularly interesting and compares the goods they offer for dyeing hair, curing freckles and restoring faded complexions with advertisements for cosmetics in her mother's magazine.

Children of all ages love stories. They are particularly

interested in personal stories and stories about the places they know. They have an aptitude for recognising the authentic, and stories of real people and real events are firm favourites. Jane, at the age of six, would sit on Grandma's lap and demand, 'Tell me about when you were a little girl.' Grandma's memories, illustrated by odds and ends from her treasure chest, kept Jane absorbed for hours.

Peter, an avid reader at the age of seven, fed his imagination on stories of Nelson, Drake and Columbus. The Vikings stirred him in a way that tales of modern warfare failed to do. The colourful drama of other days awakened his interest in history, and the noble characters he met in it he regarded as his personal friends. Any pet he acquired was named after one of his heroes.

Andrea was given a copy of *The God of the Silver Bow*, by Cecily M. Rutley, on her eighth birthday. Although she associated Orpheus and Psyche with King Canute and characters from the *Arabian Nights*, she was convinced that these people, and others like them, really lived and that things were not always as they are today.

Stories associated with places the child knows well likewise provide a personal link with the living past. Well-established localities with old buildings, churches, castles and the like offer good starting-points for historical discovery. Nearer home, the family prayer-book preserves living evidence of those who went before. The modern home on the housing estate may have less to offer, but most localities retain points of historical interest, even if only in the names of streets.

Sunday school, with its Bible stories and poems from ancient times, is another source of material which carries the ring of truth. The popularity of Bible stories, many of which are intellectually and morally incomprehensible to the young child, can be explained in terms of their authenticity. Reality shines through, and the child feels they belong to him.

Stories of prehistoric man, of dinosaurs, pterodactyls and primitive tribes, are universal in their appeal to small children. The caveman faced with the problems of an inimical environment has much in common with the child, who is himself struggling to master his environment. He knows about wanting to make fire when the adult prohibits the use of matches. Later on in life, camping, canoeing and other activities will offer the child the challenge of mastering an environment with the aid of only simple equipment. Before that time the child enjoys this interest vicariously by reliving the struggles of early man.

The child's understanding of situations often develops through dramatic interpretation. Sometimes he may play out stories he has heard and read. Very often his play centres round archetypes. Kings and queens and princesses are rarely portrayed in modern style; the king wears velvet robes and a crown, and the prince carries a sword and rides a snow-white steed. Robin Hood is a romantic figure from the past, and his popularity has never been diminished by that of the modern gangster. In their play children tend to preserve these colourful characters from history; this kind of play also emerges in the adult world in the form of pageants and Lord Mayor's shows. These spectacular scenes, and the pageantry of such occasions as a Coronation, help to parade the past before the child and to interest him in it. Some adults attribute their enthusiasm for history simply to their love of its sense of drama, its colour and romance, which offer escape from the ostensibly drab life of today.

A study of almost any environment contains a dimension of history. A thatched cottage, a village green, perhaps with its annual fête or maypole dancing, local customs and rites, are all sources of living interest. Gravestones in cemeteries offer a wealth of material for speculation.

The weather itself is a stable and permanent link with the past, and most localities have their own tales of floods, the great freeze, or summers with sun 'hot enough to split the stones'. 'Do you remember the winter of . . .' is a starting-point for many stories.

The child will acquire in his vocabulary many words which grow in meaning when related to their historical setting. Children of eight or nine may be interested in words such as 'routed' or 'cavalier', and these words become full of meaning when the child learns about Cromwell and the Roundheads.

In the early days of childhood, a sense of history grows spontaneously, and the contrived situation has little meaning at this stage. A sense of history as information conveyed by the spoken and written word comes later, but there are many ways in which the teacher can extend the experiences offered by the home. Many teachers still think of history as a subject learned by memorising sequences of events, but it is not essential for young children to know the sequence. They can enjoy history as 'patches', in which a single situation or character is associated with a group of facts. For instance, the child may handle a mediaeval pewter plate with a hollow for salt. Consideration of its purpose can create, in the imagination, the wooden table spread with meats and wine, the uncouth modes of eating, the finger-bowls, the hungry warriors hot from battle, the wolf-dogs, the serving-maids, the minstrels and the roistering.

The teacher needs to be alert to the historical material in the child's home environment. She needs to support any interest sparked off at home with supplies of good material from museums, archives and story books. Above all, she needs to develop her own interest in history, for more is conveyed to the child by the enthusiast than in any other way. Indeed many teachers have had their interest in history aroused for the first time through investigating it with the young child.

# 19

# Curiosity and wonder

Much that the child meets is new and being experienced for the first time. He is often unable to explain what he sees and wonder comes naturally to him. Knowledge and exploration can lead him to the brink of fresh wonder, but too often 'knowledge' means pinning things down to facts, filing them away and dismissing them from the mind as questions answered.

As we grow older we order our time into precise divisions, and in so doing we leave little time for wonder to develop, because wonder cannot be planned for. It comes upon us unexpectedly, and we are rarely free enough from our own commitments to recognise and to welcome it. Wonder is part of the child's nature, and when we teach we must safeguard this precious experience for him.

As adults we tend to forget the true nature of discovery. Occasionally we find ourselves in fresh situations, perhaps in a new environment, and then we experience the half-forgotten drive of curiosity, the desire to explore one's new habitat. When we are confronted with an unfamiliar environment, or have the courage to move to one, we expend a good deal of energy finding out about it and about our new position within it. The knowledge of the new situation is linked with the need to know what we can do with it and how it will change us. A change of environment may simply mean a change in the human situation, as for instance when two people marry and need to explore the nature of a new relationship and to make the necessary changes to meet it.

The exploratory drive is perhaps the most powerful form of motivation in childhood. The child learns because he must. We can help him learn by keeping his environment a source of exploration and by providing the right kind of support and assistance. We can hinder him by making his world arid or by imposing the restrictions of our own personalities upon it, or by otherwise creating an unhelpful atmosphere.

The child's curiosity may remain curiosity or it may lead to discovery. Discovery is often associated with usage. The child may, for instance, be curious about the tap. He discovers what it is for, how it works, and what he can get out of it; this is absorbed and becomes part of his experience.

In this book we have followed children in their process of discovery, and we have been led in a number of unexpected directions. One child's curiosity about light led him into the fields of science and mathematics, painting, history and geography, reading and poetry-making; it filled him with wonder and brought him to the threshold of worship. His curiosity, leading to discovery, was a unifying agent of his learning. It proved yet again the wholeness of the child, the continuity of his growth, and the integrated nature of his understanding.

If we follow the child we do not fall into the trap of turning science merely into an analytical study of the world. We do not study the firmament simply in order to fix the stars in it, whilst forgetting the splendour of the sunset sky. We know that real education consists of a single study – the exploration of the world we've inherited and of the things which live in it. In pursuing this end we reach the heart of things and become at one with our universe. We are brought to an understanding of it as a unified whole and as an independent miracle of completeness.

We know that as teachers we provide material and reference books which will satisfy enquiry. We know, too, that this is not enough. At all times our active interest in what the child is doing is essential. We do not dismiss his exploratory experiences as 'playing about' with this and that; we share what he is doing and endeavour to reach through to his mind and to understand the thought processes shaping there.

We encourage the child to discuss his discoveries, in order to further his observation. We provide words with which he can describe his discoveries more accurately. We help the child to record his observations and to clarify his findings. We take the trouble to furnish our own minds, so that we can lead the child towards finding answers to his questions, or so that we can take him a stage further in his enquiry. We know that our own enthusiasm will help both the child and ourselves to use opportunity to the full.

Above all, we discover with the child and so keep alive between us that spirit of enquiry which will help us to preserve our sensitivity to the majesty and wonder of our living world.

In Ralph Waldo Emerson's words, 'The world globes itself in a drop of dew. The microscope cannot find the animalcule which is less perfect for being little . . . The true doctrine of omnipresence is that God reappears with all his parts in every moss and cobweb.'

# Suggestions for further reading

## List A.  *Mathematics in the Primary School*

**Adams, L. D.** *A Background to Primary School Mathematics.* Oxford University Press, 1953.

**Churchill, E. M.** *Counting and Measuring: an approach to number education in the infant school.* Routledge & Kegan Paul, 1961.

**Hogben, L.** *Man Must Measure: the wonderful world of mathematics.* Rathbone, 1955.

**Land, F. W.** *The Language of Mathematics.* John Murray, 1961.

**Lovell, K.** *The Growth of Basic Scientific and Mathematical Concepts.* University of London Press, 1961.

**Peel, E. A.** *The Pupil's Thinking.* Oldbourne, 1960.

**Schools Council for the Curriculum and Examinations.** *Mathematics in Primary Schools* (Curriculum Bulletin No. 1). HMSO, 1966.

**Smith, D. E.** *Number Stories of Long Ago.* Ginn, 1948.

**Smith, T.** *The Story of Measurement.* Series 1. Blackwell, 1955.
   1. *How measuring began.*
   2. *The yard, the foot and the inch.*
   3. *Measuring land and large spaces.*
   4. *Measuring roads and long distances.*

**Smith, T.** *The Story of Measurement.* Series 2. Blackwell, 1956.
    1. *The story of weight.*
    2. *The story of money.*
    3. *The story of capacity.*
    4. *The story of time.*

**Stern, C.** *Children Discover Arithmetic.* Harrap, 1953.

**Whittaker, D. E.** *Mathematics Through Discovery.* Teacher's book and three volumes. Harrap, 1965.

## List B.  Science in the Primary School

**Allen, G. E.** and others. *Scientific Interests in the Primary School.* National Froebel Foundation, 1960.

**A.T.C.D.E.** and others. *Science in the Primary School.* John Murray, 1959.

**Association for Science Education.** *Science for Primary Schools.*
    1. *Children learning through science.*
    2. *List of books.*
    3. *List of teaching aids.*
    4. *Materials and equipment.*

**Education, Ministry of.** *Schools and the Countryside* (Pamphlet No. 35). H M S O, 1958.

**Education, Ministry of.** *Science in the Primary School* (Pamphlet No. 42). H M S O, 1961.

**Hutchinson, M. M.** *Children as Naturalists.* Allen and Unwin, 1965.

**Lawrence, E.** and others. *Approaches to Science in the Primary School.* E S A, 1960.

## List C.  Piaget

**Brearley, M.** and **Hitchfield, E.** *A Teacher's Guide to Reading Piaget.* Routledge Paperback.

Discovering the physical world

**Isaacs, N.** *The growth of understanding in the young child: a brief introduction to Piaget's work.* ESA, 1963.

**Isaacs, N.** *New light on children's ideas of number: the work of Professor Piaget.* ESA, 1960.

**Piaget, J.** *The Child's Conception of Number.* (International Library of Psychology.) Routledge & Kegan Paul, 1952.

**Piaget, J.** *The Child's Conception of Physical Causality.* (International Library of Psychology.) Routledge & Kegan Paul, 1930.

**Piaget, J.** *The Child's Conception of the World.* (International Library of Psychology.) Routledge & Kegan Paul, 1929.

**Piaget, J.** *The Child's Construction of Reality.* (International Library of Psychology.) Routledge & Kegan Paul, 1955.

**Piaget, J.** *Judgement and Reasoning in the Child.* (International Library of Psychology.) Routledge & Kegan Paul, 1928.

**Piaget, J.** *The Language and Thought of the Child.* Routledge & Kegan Paul, 1960.

**Piaget, J.** and **Inhelder, B.** *The Child's Conception of Space.* (International Library of Psychology.) Routledge & Kegan Paul, 1956.

**Piaget, J.** and **Inhelder, B.** *The Growth of Logical Thinking from Childhood to Adolescence.* Routledge & Kegan Paul, 1958.

# Index